Rubus

Herb of the Year™ 2020

International Herb Association

Compiled and edited by Gert Coleman

This book is dedicated to an extraordinary man,
Dr. Arthur Oliver Tucker,
known to many of us as Art. Those of us who knew him were privileged to have experienced his kindness, generosity, sense of humor, boundless curiosity, and his awe-inspiring knowledge of all things herbal.

A mentor to many, he was a true Renaissance man, botanist, and Green Man; his joie de vivre was contagious and we honor him here. Art served on the board of IHA for many years and was a regular contributor to our Herb of the Year™ series.

Photo Credit: Pat Kenny

IHA HERB OF THE YEAR™

Each year the International Herb Association chooses an **Herb of the Year**™ to highlight. The Horticultural Committee evaluates possible choices based on their being outstanding in at least two of the three major categories: culinary, medicinal, and ornamental. Herbal organizations around the world work together with us to educate the public throughout the year.

Herb of the Year™ books are published annually by the

International Herb Association
P.O. Box 5667 Jacksonville, Florida 32247-5667
www.iherb.org

Copyright 2020. International Herb Association. All rights reserved. No portion of these books, text, prose, recipes, illustrations, or photography may be reproduced in any manner without written permission from the International Herb Association.

This book is intended as an informational guide. The remedies, approaches, and techniques described herein are meant to supplement, and not to be a substitute for professional medical care or treatment; please consult your health care provider.

The International Herb Association is a professional trade organization providing education, service, and development for members engaged in all aspects of the herbal industry.

ISBN: 978-0-578-64224-6

*"Uniting Herb Professionals for Growth
Through Promotion and Education"*

The International Herb Association has some of the most dedicated volunteers who keep the organization afloat, giving their time and talents to ensure that IHA continues to share herbal knowledge and connect those in the profession of herbs. We are deeply indebted to the IHA Board of Directors, the IHA Foundation members, and our webmaster. Thanks for all that you do and for caring enough to move us forward!

IHA BOARD MEMBERS
Tina Marie Wilcox, President
Pat Kenny, Vice President
Karen O'Brien, Secretary
Marge Powell, Treasurer
Gert Coleman, HOY editor
Skye Suter, Newsletter editor
Kathleen Connole
Ben Cohen
Diann Nance, Past President

IHA FOUNDATION BOARD OF TRUSTEES
Chuck Voigt, Chair
Steven Lee, Vice-Chair
Ann Sprayregen, Secretary
Marge Powell, Treasurer
Davy Dabney
Donna Frawley
Tina Marie Wilcox

WEBMASTER
Jason Ashley

Acknowledgments

Besides its delicious berries and healing leaves and root, *Rubus* offers ornamental pleasures all year with bright white flowers in spring and vivid leaves in fall. From blackberries and raspberries to thimbleberries, wineberries, and more, this juicy genus *Rubus* delivers on all fronts.

Jam-packed with articles, poems, and luscious recipes, this anthology celebrates *Rubus* as the 2020 Herb of the Year™ with a veritable village of knowledgeable experts. Be prepared for some decidedly purple prose in praise of this pretty, prickly, and practical plant!

Heartfelt thanks to **Dr. Arthur O. Tucker** and **Chuck Voigt** for teaching us the botany and cultivation of varied *Rubus'* species; to **Susan Belsinger** and **Pat Kenny** for clarifying the thorny thicket of nomenclature; and to **Kathleen Connole** for its many indigenous uses. For sharing their gardening experiences and historical knowledge, thanks to **Davy Dabney**, **Skye Suter**, and **Tina Marie Wilcox**.

Celebrated for centuries, brambleberries add flavor and color to a host of tantalizing recipes. Many thanks to **Susan Belsinger**, **Pat Crocker**, **Chefs Jemal Edwards and Brad Doles**, **Karen England**, **Donna Frawley**, **Steven Lee**, **Jim Long**, **Kathryn Mollach**, **Cooper T. Murray**, **Diann Nance**, **Karen O'Brien**, **Stephanie Parello**, **Stephanie Rose**, **Ann Sprayregen**, **Skye Suter**, **Jane Taylor**, and **Chef Nick Wright** for the many ways to celebrate *Rubus* in food and drink.

Berries, roots, seeds, and leaves, all parts of *Rubus* are used in healing. Many thanks to **Janice Cox**, **Daniel Gagnon**, **Carol Little**, **Marge Powell**, **Andrea and Matthias Reisen**, and **Jane Hawley Stevens** for untangling the facts about *Rubus* remedies and benefits.

For helping us to see multi-faceted *Rubus* in her true colors, many thanks to the talented illustrators **Pat Kenny**, **Alicia Mann**, **Alice Tangerini**, **Pam Trickett**, and **Gail Wood Miller**, and the inspiring photographers who contributed this year: **Susan Belsinger**, **Peter Coleman**, **Karen England**, **Bonny Lundy**, **Cooper T. Murray**, **Diann Nance**, **Karen O'Brien**, **Marge Powell**, **Stephanie Rose,** and **Jane Taylor**. Special thanks to **Susan Belsinger** for the cover photos and for capturing *Rubus* in every glorious phase.

Many thanks to the poets for celebrating *Rubus* in words and images: **Wilma Jozwiak, Hank Kalet, B.V. Marshall**, and **Shirley Russak Wachtel**.

Much gratitude to the second readers for cogent advice, insight, and eagle-eyed proofreading: **Susan Belsinger, Kathleen Connole, Karen O'Brien, Skye Suter**, and **Chuck Voigt**. Your vigilant efforts have made this a better book.

Deep and warm appreciation to the hard-working board and foundation members who so generously give their time, energy, and expertise to keep IHA moving forward.

It has been a distinct pleasure to work with **Heather Cohen** whose many talents include layout and public relation efforts on behalf of the IHA.

Thanks also to **Ben Cohen** for his boundless enthusiasm and guidance through the challenges of on-demand publishing.

Finally, many thanks to my husband **Peter** for his photos, sense of humor, and technical support.

~Gert Coleman, Editor

A blackberry is red when it's green.
A blueberry is ripe when it's blue.
How can you know when you look down below
if a dewberry don't or it do?
Carolyn Jones

'Baby Cakes' Blackberries. *Stephanie Rose*

Table of Contents

Acknowledgments vi

Growing Rubus
Distant Relations 3
    B.V. Marshall
The Brambles: A View from a Neo-Batologist 5
    Auther O. Tucker
The Brambles: Sorting Through the Thicket of *Rubus* Terminology 13
    Susan Belsinger and Pat Kenny
Hints for a Would-Be Bramble Tamer 29
    Charles E. Voigt
Food and Medicine: Indigenous Peoples' Use of *Rubus* 39
    Kathleen Connole

Knowing Rubus
Product of Mexico 55
    Hank Kalet
Blackberry Magic: A Game of Thorns 57
    Gert Coleman
Chasing the Wild Thimbleberry: *Rubus parviflorus* 69
    Davy Dabney
Rubus and Shakers of the Herbal World 73
    Skye Suter
My Ruckus with *Rubus*: Rooting Out Invasive Plants 83
    Tina Marie Wilcox

Eating Rubus
Berry Month 91
    Wilma Jozwiak
Just Desserts 93
    Susan Belsinger
        Peach and Blackberry Crumble 93

Chocolate Shortcakes with Cocoa Whipped Cream
and Raspberries 94
Summer Berry Trifle with Lemon Herb Syrup 96
Raspberry Recipes for Any Time of Day 99
Gert Coleman
Raspberry Muffins with Pecan Streusel Topping 99
Ceil's Raspberry Bread Pudding 101
German Apple-Berry Pancake 102
Summer Easy Berry-Nut Chocolate Dessert 103
Brambleberry Bumble 105
Pat Crocker
Red Raspberry: My Favorite Fruit 107
Donna Frawley
Raspberry Vinegar 110
Salad with Creamy Raspberry Vinaigrette 110
Mixed Greens with Warm Raspberry Dressing 111
No-Churn Raspberry Ice Cream 111
Raspberry Ice 112
Chasing the Wild Berry: Chiggers, Thorns, and Ticks, Oh My! 115
Stephen Lee
Chicken in Red Berry Vinegar Sauce 118
Wild Blackberry Hand Pie 120
Wild Berry and Banana Overnight Oats 122
Two Raspberry Salsa Recipes 125
Jim Long
Raspberry Salsa 125
Raspberry Mango Salsa 126
Creme de la Crop: *Rubus* Rules 127
Cooper T. Murray
Grilled Flatbread Pizza with Blackberries
and Arugula 127
Salad with Nectarines and Blackberry Vinaigrette 130
Raspberry and Basil Chicken 131
Roasted Raspberry Chipotle Shrimp Skewers 133
Marionberry Herb Galette 134

Berries for the 4th of July 137
    Diann Nance
        Double-Crusted Berry Cobbler 139
Rich *Rubus* Berries: Terra's Transient Treasures 141
    Stephanie Parello
        Raspberry/Blackberry Coulis 141
        Raspberry-Basil Balsamic Vinaigrette 142
        Berries and Ricotta 143
Capture Summer Fresh with Blackberries 145
    Stephanie Rose
        Low-Sugar Blackberry Jam 145
        Sugar-Free Blackberry Jam with Stevia 147
Shaker Recipes for a Lavish Friday Dinner with *Rubus* 149
    Skye Suter
        Refreshing Raspberry Punch 150
        Ruby Soup 151
        Red, White and Blackberry Salad 152
        Piquant Raspberry Sauce 153
        Seasonal Vegetables with Hot Raspberry Sauce 154
        Apple Berry Pie with Rosewater 155
Rubus Tips from the Top of Manhattan 157
    Ann Sprayregen
        Raspberry BBQ Sauce 158
        Raspberry Mousse with Almond Cake 159
        Chocolate Raspberry Tart 161
Some Brambleberry Adventures for Family, Food and Fun! 165
    Jane L. Taylor
        Brambleberry Cookies 167
        Brambleberry Fairy Cakes 169
        Blackberry Fool 171
        Toad Hall Trifle 172
        Toad in the Hole with Jam Toasts 173
        Thumbprint Cookies 175
        Green Gables Raspberry Cordial 176
        Blackberry or Raspberry Simple Syrup 177
        Blackberry Ink 179

Drinking Rubus

Will You 185
    Shirley Russak Wachtel

Rubus Infusions 187
    Susan Belsinger
        Simply *Rubus* 188
        Cheers to Your Health 189
        Really Rosy *Rubus* Infusion 190

Rubus Smoothies: It's the Berries! 193
    Pat Crocker
        Black Belt Smoothie 194
        Berry Yogurt Flip Smoothie 195
        Best Berries Smoothie 195
        Berry Blast Smoothie 196
        Berry Bonanza Smoothie 196
        California Cup Smoothie 197
        Black Currant-Blackberry Smoothie 197
        Berries and Cream Smoothie 198

Cocktails, Anyone? 201
    Karen England
        Bramble 203
        Ramble 204
        Dramble 204
        Homemade Organic Blackberry or Raspberry Liqueur
            Ala' Creme de Mure 205
        Herbal Honey Simple Syrup 206

Wild Blackberry Brandy 207
    Kathryn Mollach

Drinking Your Raspberry: Making Liqueurs and Infused Beverages 209
    Karen O'Brien
        Raspberry Liqueur 211
        Two Berry Vodka 212
        Blackberry Brandy 213
        Kir Royale *Rubus* 213
        Peach Melba-Raspberry Sangria 214
        Floral Ice Wreath 215

Raspberry Shrub 215
Bracing *Rubus* Beverages 219
    Stephanie Parello
        Raspberry Bay Lemonade 219
        Blackberry Bracer 220
Berry Garden Mixology 221
    Stephanie Rose
        Wild Blackberry Cordial 221
        Blackberrycello 222
Manhattan Berry Mixology 223
    Chef Nick Wright
        Smoky Raspberry Margarita 223

Healing Rubus

Ode To Blackberries 227
    Gert Coleman
Natural Beauty with *Rubus* 229
    Janice Cox
        Blackberry Antioxidant Facial Mask 230
        Raspberry Leaf Astringent 230
        Fresh Berry Cleanser 231
        Rubus Leaf Mouth Rinse 231
        Blackberry Leaf Hair Rinse 232
        Simple Berry Lip Gloss 233
Medicinal Uses of Raspberry and Blackberry 235
    Daniel Gagnon
Raspberry Medicine 249
    Carol Little
Raspberry Soother Balm 255
    Marge Powell
In the Briar Patch with Blackberry 261
    Andrea and Matthias Reisen
Pay Attention to *Rubus*: She Wants to Help! 265
    Jane Hawley Stevens
Bios for Illustrators and Photographers 271
Cover Credits 273
Herb of the Year™ Selection 274
Join the IHA 275

Growing Rubus

Blackberry 'Baby Cakes' flower. *Pat Kenny*

Distant Relations

B.V. Marshall

Is the wild rose in the front yard truly related
to the even wilder berry in the back? Are they
the Sadie and Maud of their own cottage plantation?

The rambling bramble, that shy rubus, never leaves
the weedy patch near the rear fence by the stoic garage.
Sadie Berry's indispensable with her offerings, those small,

Jewel-toned drupelets, lush and plump and roundly red
above her thorns. "Take these from me,"
she seems to say. "Get them before the crows come."

Yet the wily deer and nimble bird manage to feast
on her gifts before the day's begun. But is the shrub
by the front door merely a stranger or truly a distant cousin?

Maddening Maude, world traveler, adored in damask,
forever in youthful bud, she's hybridized beyond recognition.
We overlook her piercing barbs. They are

as unexpected as a thunderstorm at dawn.
Hers are gentle petals and bee-pleasing perfume that lasts
only an evening. Such transient beauty,

she forgot where she came from. Maude Rose and
Sadie Berry lie on different places on the same land.
This is the divide that's biblical and humble.

This is the stuff of brocaded novels with
rivalries as deep as roots that's covered in muck.
They both bear their flower and fruit with thorns.

It is such a large family when one sister does not know
the existence of the other in her own back yard.

Field-grown wild blackberry. *Peter Coleman*

B. V. Marshall's plays have earned recognition from HBO New Writers Workshop, New York's Theatre for a New City, Chicago's public radio station WBEZ, and in play festivals from Alaska to Australia. Awards include Playwriting Fellowships from NJ Council on the Arts, the Geraldine R. Dodge Foundation, VCCA, NEH, and the Robert Chesle-Victor Bumbalo foundation. Most recently he received the 2018 Stanley Drama Award for *Incident at Willow Creek*. After studying playwriting at Hunter University, he earned an MFA in Creative Writing from the University of Massachusetts Amherst. B. V. Marshall is a member of the Dramatists Guild, New Play Exchange, and the 9th Floor. He is an Associate Professor of English at Middlesex County College, New Jersey.

The Brambles: A View from a Neo-Batologist

Arthur O. Tucker

Rubus
Family: Rosaceae

Growth form: shrub with prostrate to upright canes, scraggly, often armed

Hardiness: variable, from arctic to tropical, from alpine to lowland

Light: full to part sun

Water: variable, but most species prefer moist but well-drained soil

Soil: variable, but most species prefer a soil rich in organic matter

Propagation: rooting of tips of arching canes (layering), some underground shoots, seeds

Culinary and medicinal use: many species have edible fruit and are rich in antioxidants, leaves brewed into teas, fruits yield good natural pigments for food coloring

Craft use: limited, pigments

Landscape use: some ground covers, double-flowered forms are very rose-like and ornamental

Rubus is derived the Latin *ruber,* meaning "red," referring to the color of the fruit of many species (and sometimes the stems). *Batologist* is derived from the Greek *báton* (blackberry) and means "one who studies brambles." Common names of the genus include raspberries, blackberries, and dewberries. Most of the species are armed with prickles (epidermal outgrowths) like roses,

Drupelets ripening in Art Tucker's raspberry patch. *Susan Belsinger*

along with spines (modified leaves) and glandular hairs, often colored red or bronze. The growth of brambles (sometimes termed *briars* or *briers*) is very typical, with the growth of a new cane (*primocane*) in year one, which then yields blossoms and fruit in the following year (*floricane*) and then dies, only to be replaced with new canes for the following year. The fruit, alias bramble fruit, is actually an aggregate of smaller fruits called drupes (*drupelets*), and the terms *cane fruit* or *cane berries* can be applied to the entire genus. Modern breeding has produced many hybrid berries, such as loganberry, boysenberry, veitchberry, skellyberry, marionberry, silvanberry, tayberry, tummelberry, and hildaberry.

With abundant polyploidy, hybridization, and facultative apomixes (able to set seed without fertilization), the number of species in the genus *Rubus* is anyone's guess, as one taxonomist's species is another taxonomist's subspecies or *varietas* with differing viewpoints on the weight of morphology versus molecular evidence. This is especially difficult in the subgenus *Rubus*. The best guess is a range, from 200 to 700 species. To confuse matters even further, *Rubus* exhibits an unusual meiosis, resulting in unexpected chromosome numbers in the progeny known as *complement fractionation*. This confuses Mendelian inheritance with multiples of recessive and dominant genes, resulting in unexpected variation (sometimes termed *transgressive hybridization*) that exceeds the parents. Breeding the brambles is frustrating but fascinating!

The genus *Rubus* has been used since antiquity; Hummer (2010) published an excellent summary of its medicinal use through the early 21st century:

> The genus *Rubus* L., indigenous to six continents, includes blackberries, raspberries, and their hybrids and is commonly referred to as brambles or briers. *Rubus* species were a food and medicinal source for native peoples soon after the Ice Age. This short article presents only a sample of the wealth of historical reports of medicinal uses for *Rubus*. Brambles were documented in the writings of the ancient Greeks: Aeschylus, Hippocrates, Krataeus, Dioscorides, and Galen; Romans: Cato, Ovid, and Pliny the Elder; Asian medicinal traditions; traditional Chinese medicine; and the Ayurvedic tradition of India. Folk traditions of native peoples throughout the world have also applied *Rubus* for multiple medicinal uses. Although in modern times *Rubus* is grown for its delicious and vitamin-rich fruit for fresh and processed product consumption, the ancients used the whole plant and its parts. Stems, branches, roots, leaves, and flowers were used in decoctions, infusions, plasters, oil

or wine extractions, and condensates. Decoctions of branches were applied to stop diarrhea, dye hair, prevent vaginal discharge, and as an antivenom for snakebites. Leaves were chewed to strengthen gums and plastered to constrain shingles, head scurf, prolapsed eyes, and hemorrhoids. Flowers triturated with oil reduced eye inflammations and cooled skin rashes; infusions with water or wine aided stomach ailments. Greeks and Romans recorded female applications, whereas the Chinese described uses in male disorders. The fruits of *R. chingii* are combined in a yang tonic called *fu pen zi,* "overturned fruit bowl," and prescribed for infertility, impotence, low backache, poor eyesight, and bedwetting or frequent urination. *The Leechbook of Bald* described the use of brambles against dysentery, combining ancient medicinal knowledge with pagan superstition and herb lore. Medicinal properties of *Rubus* continue in Renaissance and modern herbals, sanctioning leaf infusions as a gargle for sore mouth, throat cankers, and as a wash for wounds; the bark, containing tannin, was a tonic for diarrhea; and root extract, a cathartic and emetic. Recent research has measured high ellagic acid, anthocyanin, total phenolics, and total antioxidant content in *Rubus* fruits. Fruit extracts have been used as colorants and are now being tested as anticarcinogenic, antiviral, antiallergenic, and cosmetic moisturizing compounds. From ancient traditions through conventional folk medicines to the scientific confirmation of health-promoting compounds, *Rubus* is associated with health-inducing properties.

Turning to the New World, *R. adenotrichus* Schltdl., tropical highland blackberry, is discussed on folio 54 of the Codex Cruz-Badianus from 1552 in New Spain as *to[h]toloctzin,* an ingredient to remove the "fetid odor of the infirm."

In a comparison of blueberries, black currant, blackberries, and black raspberries, black raspberry cultivars have the highest total anthocyanin content. This is particularly important because not only are these anthocyanins good antioxidants, but they may be beneficial against several types of human cancer. Every day should include one of the small, colored berries in your diet!

Modern medicinal use is primarily centered upon the European blackberry as an herbal medicine. The correct name of this species is often applied to an aggregate of species of subgenus *Rubus* section *Rubus* and best characterized simply as *R. fruticosus* auct. (*auctoris*, "of authors"). This aggregate of

Rubus pentalobus 'Sonya's parasol.' *Karen O'Brien*

species has been shown to be antimicrobial, anticarcinogenic, antidysentery, antidiabetic, antidiarrheal, and also a good antioxidant. Not only are the berries used for medicine, but also the leaves, stems, and even roots. Blackberry leaf tea is sometimes offered, but my favorite is black iced tea mixed with a touch of bramble juice and a squeeze of fresh lemon juice.

Looking at the landscape potential, my spring garden cannot be without the abundant white, rose-like flowers of the double *R. rosifolius* Sm. 'Coronarius.' For over forty years it has flourished under the dappled shade near a pine tree, occasionally putting up underground shoots to share. I've always wanted to try the other double brambles, such as the pale pink *R. ulmifolius* Schott 'Bellidiflorus' or the dark pink *R. spectabilis* Pursh 'Olympic Double.' Even the single magenta-flowering *R. odoratus* L. is attractive. At the top of my rockery, *R. pentalobus* Hayata (*R. calycinoides* Hayata) has provided a tight groundcover with roundish green leaves often edged in bronze.

European Blackberry
Rubus fruticosus
rŭ-bəs fru-tí-cō-sus

Rubus fruticosis is an ambiguous name that derives its scientific name from the Latin *frutex*, "bush or shrub."

Botanical Description
R. fruticosus auct.
Native country: Europe, naturalized worldwide
General habit: shrub with canes
Leaves: deciduous, usually palmately compound
Flowers: five white petals in a terminal inflorescence, occasionally magenta, rarely double
Fruits/Seeds: small brown seeds contained within drupelets

References

Bammi, R. K. 1965. 'Complement fractionation' in a natural hybrid between *Rubus procerus* Muell. and *R. laciniatus* Willd. *Nature* 208:608.

Hummer, K. E. 2010. *Rubus* pharmacology: antiquity to the present. *HortScience* 45:1587-1591.

_____, and J. Janick. 2007. *Rubus* iconography: Antiquity to the Renaissance. *Acta Hort.* 759:90-105.

Jennings, D. L., D. L. Craig, and P. B. Topham. 1967. The role of the male parent in the reproduction of *Rubus*. *Heredity* 22:43-55.

Moyer, R. A., K. E. Hummer, C. E. Finn, B. Frei, and R. E. Wrolstad. 2002. Anthocyanins, phenolics, and antioxidant capacity in diverse small fruits: *Vaccinium, Rubus,* and *Ribes*. *J. Agric. Food Chem.* 50:519-525.

Seeram, N. P. 2008. Berry fruits: Compositional elements, biochemical activities, and the impact of their intake on human health, performance, and disease. *J. Agric. Food Chem.* 56:627-629.

Thompson, M. M. 1962. Cytogenetics of *Rubus*. III. Meiotic instability in some higher polyploids. *Amer. J. Bot.* 49:575-582.

Verma, R., T. Gangrade, R. Punasiya, and C. Ghulaxe. 2014. *Rubus fruticosus* (blackberry) use as an herbal medicine. *Pharmacognosy Rev.* 8(16):101-104.

Dr. Arthur O. Tucker authored numerous scientific and popular publications, including, with Thomas DeBaggio, *The Encyclopedia of Herbs* (Timber 2009), *Herbs of Commerce* (APHA 2000), and, with Susan Belsinger, *The Culinary Herbal* (Taunton 2015). Retired from Delaware State University where he taught botany, especially the identification and chemistry of plants of flavor, fragrance, and medicine, Art inspired countless students and herbalists to grow healthier plants, bring in better harvests, and simply enjoy herbal flavors and fragrances more fully. Art served on the IHA board for many years with humor, dignity and enthusiasm. He is much missed.

Rubus fruticosus 'Chester' thornless. *Pat Kenny*

The Brambles: Sorting through the Thicket of *Rubus* Terminology

Susan Belsinger and Pat Kenny

Delving deeply into this subject, we have found that there are many botanical terms that we feel necessary to better define—so that is our task here—with Pat's detailed illustrations and our joint *Rubus* research. Our subjects, *Rubus* spp., members of the Rosaceae, are a prickly bunch commonly referred to as brambles or brambleberries, and sometimes caneberries.

According to https://www.britannica.com/plant/bramble: "Bramble, (genus *Rubus*), large genus of flowering plants in the rose family (Rosaceae), consisting of usually prickly shrubs. Brambles occur naturally throughout the world, especially in temperate areas, and a number are invasive species outside their native range. Many are widely cultivated for their fruits, including raspberries, blackberries, and hybrids such as loganberries and boysenberries."

Although some species are herbaceous, most of these shrubs have erect, canelike stems, which are somewhat woody, with prickles, bristles, and gland-tipped hairs, although some are hybridized to get rid of the prickles and bristles and are sold as thornless (most or all of these are spontaneous thornless chimeras, which are propagated to maintain this condition). In the wild, the canes of *Rubus* bend and arc, while cultivated canes are commonly grown with supports, such as wires or a trellis.

While some species have simple leaves, other species have the familiar characteristics of alternate compound leaves, 3 to 7 leaflets, and often stipules. The five-petaled flowers (look similar to a wild rose) are most often white, though some are pale pink, and sometimes an even darker shade of pink. These blooms have many stamens attached to a calyx; sepals of the blackberry group fold down, whereas those of the raspberry stretch out.

Eventually flowers develop into berries, which are technically an aggregate of drupelets.

Rubus befuddles most botanists because it hybridizes so easily, resulting in a large and diverse genus with 250 to 700 species; it often makes identification challenging. Many species reproduce vegetatively by tip-rooting; some propagate by suckering from stolon runners or rhizomes.

How do you tell a raspberry from a blackberry?

There are a few different ways (fruit, leaf and cane) to identify the difference between raspberries (*Rubus idaeus* L.) and blackberries (*Rubus fruticosus* L.), however, the easiest and most obvious way is how the berries come off the plant. When raspberries, as well as black raspberries (*R. occidentalis*) and wineberries (*R. phoenicolasius*), are picked, their stems and receptacles (also called torus, plural tori) stay on the plant and the berries are hollow. Blackberries keep their stems when picked and the berries have a center receptacle, so they are not hollow.

A few other differentiations are that blackberries grow much taller than raspberries—they can reach up to 10 feet in height—while raspberries grow about 4 to 6 feet tall. In general, blackberries have thicker stems and prickles and raspberries have thinner stems and prickles with black raspberries in the middle-size range.

The foliage is also an identifier: blackberry leaves are green on both sides, while the green leaves of raspberry and black raspberry have whitish undersides.

Generally, black raspberries ripen first in early summer, followed by raspberries in mid-summer and the blackberries are last to bear fruit in late summer.

Raspberry, hollow, receptacle left on plant   Blackberry, retains receptacle

What is the difference between thorns, spines and prickles?

People are often surprised to find that those really aren't thorns on those brambles—rose bushes, raspberries and blackberries; those sharp points that prick you are prickles. Here's a fairly simple definition from an article titled "Difference between Thorns, Spines, and Prickles": "Key Difference: In plant morphology, thorns, spines and prickles are all similar type of structures identified by their sharp and stiff ends. Thorns are obtained from shoots. Spines are obtained from leaves and prickles are derived from the epidermis. They all are related to anti-herbivore defense mechanisms of plants.

"… One must not consider thorns, spines and prickles to be the same thing. Thorns are modified branches or stems. Spines are modified leaves and prickles are simply extension of the plant cortex and epidermis. Unlike spines, thorns are deeply seated and have connection with vascular tissues. Thorns are formed from deeply seated tissues of the plant. On the other hand, spines are formed from tissues present externally."

Here are a few more points that we found useful in defining the difference between thorns and prickles, published by Indiana Public Media, Moments of Science Staff: "Thorns, like those found on the Hawthorn tree, are modified branches that project from the stem and branches of a woody plant. They are very sharp, and quite strong as they are made of the same stuff as the stem of the tree or bush. Thorns are deeply embedded in the woody structure of the plant, and can't be broken off easily. Those nasty points on the stem of the rose are not, in fact, true thorns, but are what scientists call prickles.

"Prickles are small, sharp outgrowths of the plant's outer layers, or skin-like epidermis, and the sub-epidermal layer just beneath it. Unlike a thorn, a prickle can be easily broken off the plant because it is really a feature of the outer layers rather than part of the wood, like a thorn."

Somehow the old saying "a rose between two thorns" just doesn't sound quite as emphatic as "a rose between two prickles."

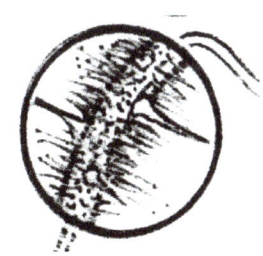

Close-up of prickles and glandular hairs

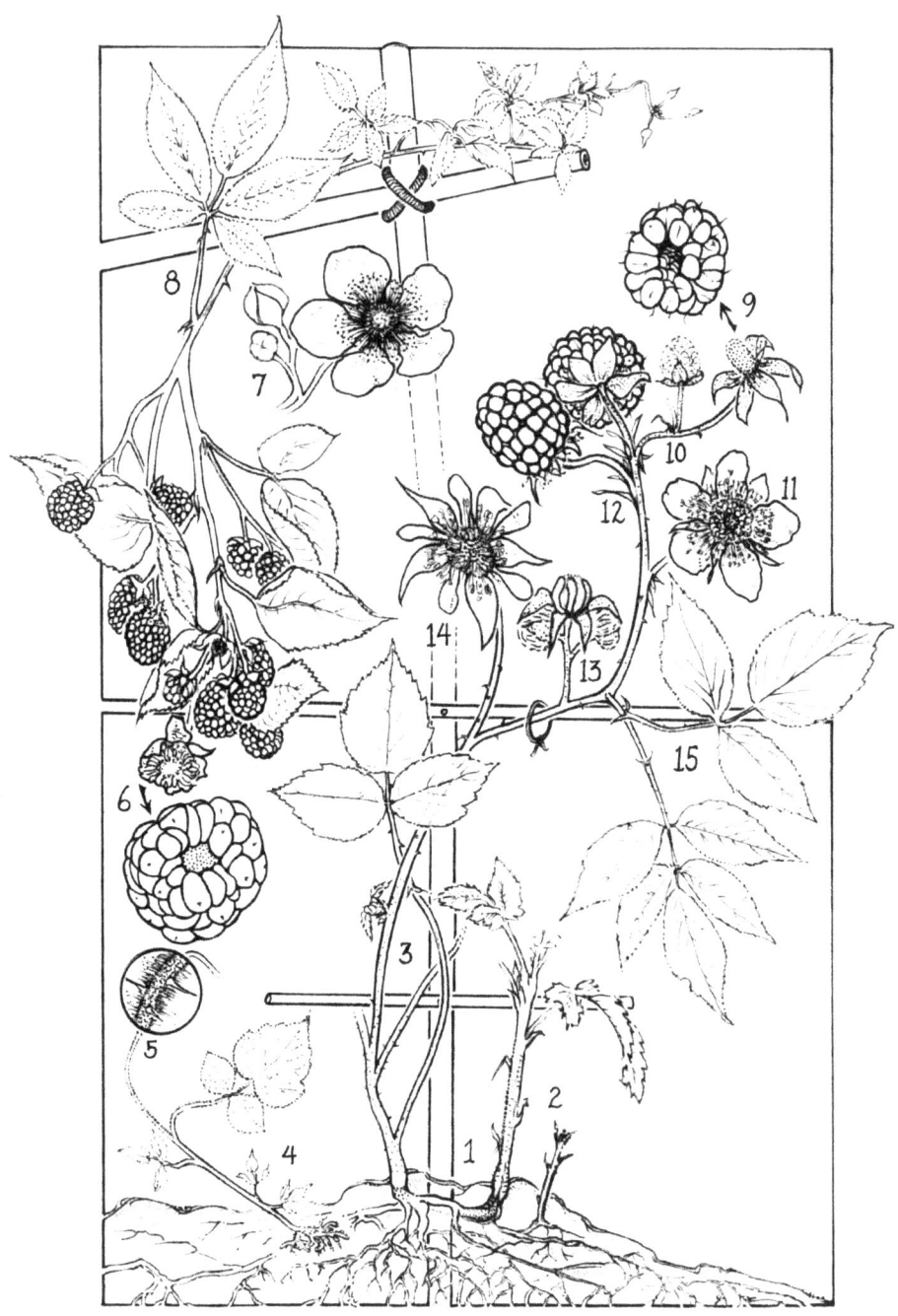

Composite Schematic Drawing of *Rubus* spp.

1. Shoot development from root buds in the crown
2. Primocanes
3. Floricanes
4. Typical tip-rooting; here in the aggressive wineberry.
5. Enlargement of typical wineberry stem showing prickles and bristles; we added gland-tipped hairs which may be found on young calyces of buds.
6. Blackberry comes off pedicel containing receptacle; see remains of stamens and calyx.
7. Typical rendition of blackberry flower
8. Typical blackberry leaf, *Rubus fruticosus*
9. Raspberry comes off leaving receptacle, (also referred to as knob or torus) on pedicel.
10. Young fruit
11. Typical raspberry flower
12. Peduncle of a cluster of *Rubus* fruits
13. Young black raspberry cluster of buds
14. Typical black raspberry flower and leaf
15. Typical raspberry leaves

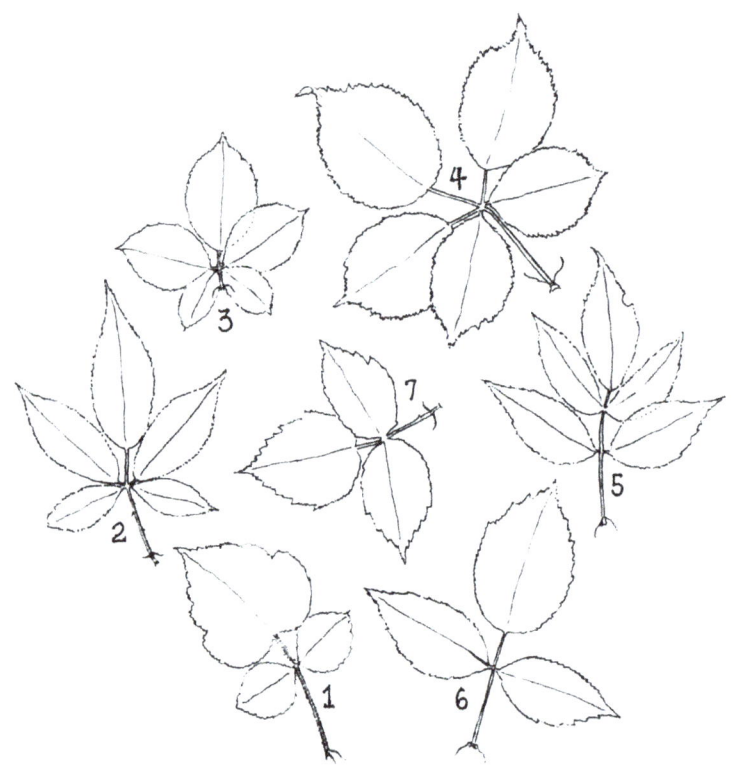

Different *Rubus* Leaves
(note stipules on petiole ends)

1. *Rubus phoenicolasius* Wineberry
2. *R. fruticosus* Blackberry
3. *R. fruticosus* 'Baby Cakes'
4. *R. fruticosus* 'Chester', said to be "thornless" (smooth stems, no emergences)
5. *R. idaeus* 'Carolina Red' raspberry
6. *R. idaeus* 'Carolina Red' raspberry
7. *R. occidentalis* Black raspberry

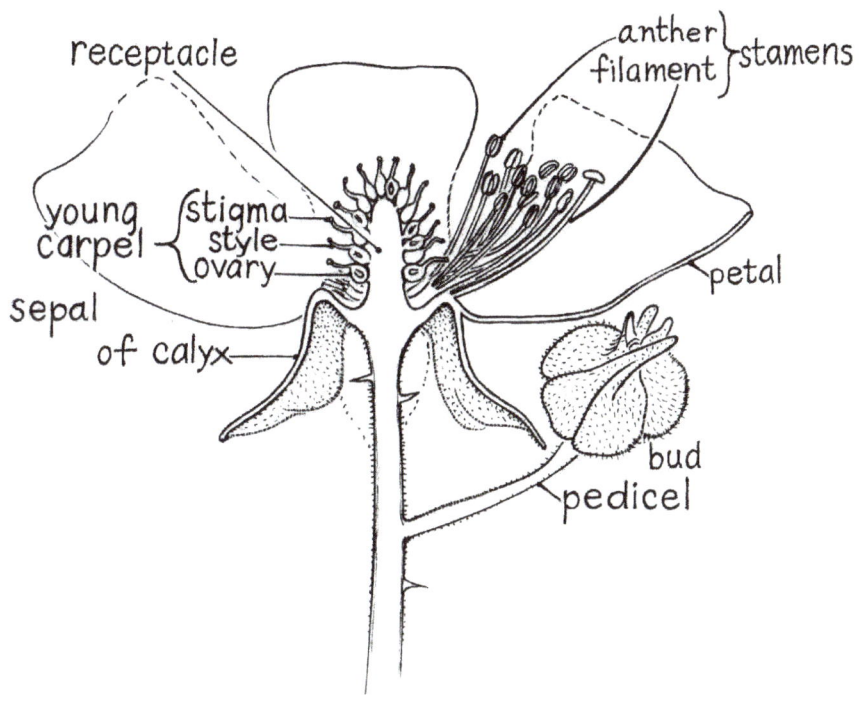

Detailed Flower Parts

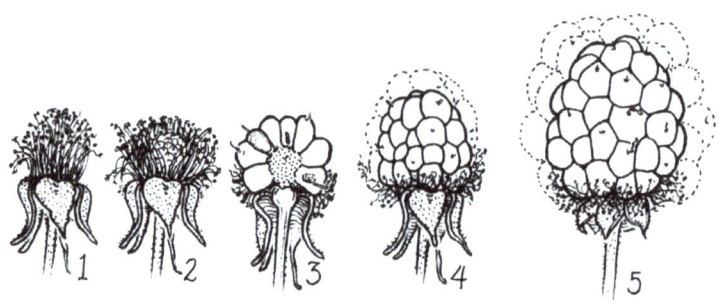

Blackberry Development Sequence
(inspired by photographs on pages 40 to 41 in *The Visual Dictionary of Plants*)

1. Fertilization has taken place; petals fall off.

2. Ovaries begin to swell; stamens wither and die.

3. Longitudinal section shows carpels or pericarps are forming (exocarp = skin, mesocarp = flesh, endocarp = a hard, inner layer, pyrenes within).

4. Carpels mature into drupelets (small fleshy fruits with single seeds surrounded by hard endocarp) then mesocarp of drupelet becomes larger, darker and sweeter (dotted line).

5. Note remains of styles of ovaries and remains of stamens in fully ripened aggregate of drupelets (dotted line) which become even larger.

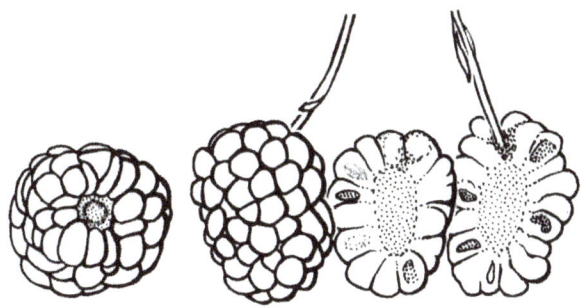

Whole ripe blackberry off calyx

and unripe blackberry longitudinally cut through,
still on pedicel. Note dotted receptacle (torus or knob)
and different visuals of seeds (pyrenes), some not viable.

A bucket of just-picked wineberries is one of the pleasures of summer.
Susan Belsinger

Glossary

Anther—the expanded, apical (apical means located at the tip or apex) part of the stamen, which contains the pollen, usually found in the center of a bloom.

Bramble—a shrub or vine of the rose family that has prickly canes or stems; an English term often used to describe plants of the genus *Rubus*, such as raspberries and blackberries.

Bristle—a sharp and short, stiff hair or hairlike structure on a plant.

Calyx—the outer whorl surrounding the perianth of a flower, it envelops the base of a flower, which includes all of the sepals.

Cane—long and slender woody stem that is not very rigid of blackberries or raspberries.

Chimera—a plant or part of a plant, which is a combination of two or more genetically different cell types.

Compound leaf—a leaf composed of several leaflets.

Drupe—a fleshy fruit usually having a single, hard, nutlike seed, like a cherry, olive or peach.

Drupelet—a small drupe, one small segment in an aggregate fruit like raspberries or blackberries, each tiny drupelet or drupel contains a seed surrounded by flesh.

Emergence—standing out or rising from.

Filament—the threadlike stalk of a stamen which bears the anther.

Floricane—second-year cane of *Rubus* which flowers and fruits.

Glandular hair—a thin, hairlike protuberance bearing or resembling glands, which may secrete a substance, usually sticky or oily.

Leaflet—a small leaf, or one of the divisions of a compound leaf.

Lobed—having a lobe or lobes (a segment or separation up to halfway to the center of a leaf).

Ovary—the enlarged, usually basal part of the pistil, which contains the ovules (immature seed) that eventually become the fruit.

Petiole—the stalk that attaches the leaf to the stem; petiolate means having a petiole.

Pistil—the female reproductive organ of a flower; usually has three parts: ovary, style and stigma. Pistillate refers to having a pistil or having a pistil with non-functioning stamens.

Prickle—a small, sharp spinelike point or outgrowth coming from the epidermis or bark of a plant, not from the wood; also referred to as an emergence. Prickles can occur on leaf veins, margins or bracts and even on fruits.

Primocane—first-year cane of *Rubus* which usually does not flower.

Pyrene—the small hard nutlet or stone of a drupe or drupelet; an endocarpic seed.

Receptacle—the expanded portion of the stem of a flower upon which the reproductive parts are borne; also referred to as a knob or torus (plural tori) which is a more specific, proper term, whereas receptacle is more common.

Simple leaf—a singular leaf.

Spine—a sharp-pointed outgrowth of a stem (like on a hawthorn tree); it is a modified leaf or stipule (one of a pair of leaflike lateral appendages at the base of a petiole).

Stamen—the pollen-bearing, male reproductive organ of a flower having two parts: filament and anther.

Stigma—the part of the pistil of a flower, which is receptive to the pollen and from which it germinates, most often located on the tip of the ovary or style.

Stipule—one of a pair of leaflike lateral appendages at the base of a petiole.

Style—most often, the narrowest part of the pistil which connects the ovary to the stigma.

Toothed—having leaf margins that are serrated; not smooth.

Torus—the expanded portion of the stem of a flower upon which the reproductive parts are borne; also referred to as a receptacle or knob. Torus (plural tori) is a more specific, proper term, whereas receptacle is a more common term.

Thorn—a rigid, sharp, pointed modified stem which is projected from the stems or branches of woody plants; it can be identified because it is subtended by a leaf.

Ripening wineberry aggregates. Note bare, orange receptacle where berry was picked. *Susan Belsinger*

Sources for Research and Drawings

Applequist, Wendy, illustrated by Barbara Alongi. *The Identification of Medicinal Plants–A Handbook of the Morphology of Medicinal Botanicals in Commerce.* Missouri Botanical Garden Press in collaboration with American Botanical Council, 2006.

Bell, Adrian D., illustrated by Alan Bryan. *Plant Forms–An Illustrated Guide to Flowering Plant Morphology.* Oxford Press, 1991.

"Bramble." *Encyclopedia Britanica.* Accessed 8/21/19. https://www.britannica.com/plant/bramble.

Dalaba Justin. "Brambleberries: What's the Difference?" *Nature Up North,* 7/15/15. Accessed 7/30/19. https://natureupnorth.org/justmynature/justindalaba/brambleberries-whats-difference.

"Development of Fruits." *SlideShare.* Accessed 5/19/19. https://www.slideshare.net/zssi/fruits-development.

"Difference between Thorns, Spines, and Prickles." *Difference Between.* Accessed 6/24/19. http://www.differencebetween.info/difference-between-thorns-spines-and-prickles.

Dowden, Anne Ophelia, illustrated by the author. *From Flower to Fruit.* Thomas Y. Crowell, 1984.

Elpel, Thomas J., illustrated by the author. *Botany In A Day-- The Patterns Method of Plant Identification–An Herbal Field Guide to Plant Families of North America.* HOPS Press, 2013.

Falconi, Dina, illustrated by Wendy Hollender. *Foraging and Feasting–A Field Guide and Wild Foods Cookbook.* Botanical Arts Press, 2013.

Glass, Don. "A Rose By Any Other Name." *A Moment of Science,* 1/18/19. Accessed 6/30/19. https://indianapublicmedia.org/amomentofscience/a-rose-by-any-other-name/.

"Growing Blackberries in Your Home Garden." *OSU Extension Catalog.* Accessed 7/15/19. https://catalog.extension.oregonstate.edu/ec1303/html.

Harris, James G. and Melinda Woolf Harris, illustrated by the authors. *Plant Identification Terminology–An Illustrated Glossary.* Spring Lake Publ, 1994.

Hill, Lewis and Leonard Perry. *The Fruit Gardener's Bible.* Storey, 2011.

Holmes, Roger, ed. *Taylor's Guide to Fruits and Berries.* Houghton Mifflin, 1996.

Lindsay, Mary, Project Editor, and Chez Picthall, Art Director. *The Visual Dictionary of Plants–An Eyewitness Dictionary.* Dorling Kindersley, 1992.

Lura, Stefan B. Staff botanist for the U.S. National Arboretum,

Washington, D.C. gave essential help with the technical details in writings and drawings.

Philip Lief Group, Inc. *National Gardening Association Dictionary of Horticulture.* Penguin Books, 1994.

"Plant Classification, Anatomy, & Function." Accessed 7/21/19. http://www.cobalt-group.com/frontpagewebs/Content/Classify/classifi.htm.

"Raspberry Care and Cultivation." *Vegetable Garden Reference Center.* Accessed 7/31/19. https://luv2garden.com/raspberries.html. WIKIpedia—photographic image sites of various members of the *Rubus* genus.

"Wineberry: The Edible Invasive." *The Infinite Spider,* 7/1/16. Accessed 7/11/19. https://infinitespider.com/wineberry-the-edible-invasive/.

Zomlefer, Wendy B., illustrated by the author. *Guide to Flowering Plant Families.* U of North Carolina Press, 1994.

Retired medical illustrator **Pat Kenny** turns from drawing the innards of *Homo sapiens* to those of plants. Not an artist but a graphic technician with a small knowledge of how to see-hand-draw in the garden and look stuff up in books and on the internet, she tries to copy enough of a plant to further her understanding, and perhaps help others to do the same.

Susan Belsinger looks forward to each new Herb of the Year™ and getting to know them intimately. She enjoys immersing herself in cultivating, researching, photographing—and creating delicious dishes to eat, beverages to imbibe, and condiments for the pantry—as well as every other aspect, be they for health and well-being, spa herbs or getting crafty. The best part is sharing the experiences and knowledge with other like-minded people.

Wild bramble canes in spring, just leafing out. *Susan Belsinger*

Hints for a Would-Be Bramble Tamer

Charles E. Voigt

Introduction

Although called *berries*, all members of the genus *Rubus* bear aggregate fruit, not true botanical berries such as blueberries, cranberries, and (yes) tomatoes. These aggregates are composed of numerous drupelets arranged around the receptacle, or *torus,* and adhering together into a unified fruit. In raspberries, the fruit detaches from the torus when picked at ripeness, leaving it behind on the plant. For blackberries, the torus adheres to the fruit at ripeness and remains a part of the harvested fruit. Fortunately, the torus is soft and easily chewable in blackberries.

In their native state, *Rubus* species tend to form thickets, which are hard to penetrate due to the abundance of sharp prickles on the canes. Tending to grow in the same areas as poison ivy in North America adds to the difficulty of safely passing through these bramble thickets. Cultivars within this genus have been developed which have larger, more abundant, and more durable fruit. In the case of upright and semi-upright blackberries, the crossing and blending of multiple species has led to a group of cultivars collectively called *Rubus* subgenus *Rubus*.

Many chance and intentional interspecific cultivars have been named and grown. Red and black raspberry have been crossed to produce purple raspberries. Red raspberry has been selected to bear golden or yellow fruit. Blackberries and red raspberries have been hybridized to yield boysenberry, loganberry, and tayberry, known collectively as *Rubus loganobaccus.*

All commonly grown cultivars of *Rubus* grow best in humus-rich mineral soils, which are moderately fertile and reasonably well-drained. Prior to planting, perennial weeds need to be eradicated, as they will compete with and shorten the productive lifetime of the *Rubus* patch. Once the planting is established, all weeds should be promptly removed or discouraged with thick organic mulch. Raspberries thrive best at pH readings of 5.6 to 6.5 while blackberries have a wider range of tolerance to pH values from 4.5 to 7.5.

Planting stock should be either certified disease-free or tissue culture plants. The process of cell culture can be used to produce disease-free plants with extreme vigor. Conventionally-produced disease-free plants should not have immediate disease issues but may lack the superior vigor of tissue cultured plants. Either of these should be bought from dependable, reputable sources to ensure getting what is advertised.

Irrigation of the plants may be necessary during establishment of the plants, any time there is drought stress, and especially as fruit nears ripening. The full, luscious drupelets will only develop fully with adequate soil moisture. Without enough water, the fruit can become dried out and seedy. Trickle or drip irrigation is highly desirable, since overhead irrigation will wet the fruit and greatly shorten its shelf life by encouraging softening and rot. Water on foliage will similarly encourage leaf diseases which can severely reduce productivity. Moderate amounts of fertilizer can be injected through the drip system. Commercial production for mass market fresh sales often utilizes high tunnel greenhouses or other clear-roof structures so that no rainfall or overhead irrigation can harm the fruit or the foliage.

All the common species and types feature biennial shoots or *canes*, which grow vegetatively the first year and fruit the second, after undergoing vernalization, a winter cold treatment. First-year canes are called *primocanes* and these will turn into *floricanes* the following year, producing flowers and fruit. Red raspberries and some blackberries have been selected to bear fruit on primocanes at the end of the first year's cycle without requiring a cold period to initiate flowering. These begin fruiting at the tips of the canes, then proceed downward until weather halts the growing season. Although primocane-bearing black raspberries are known to exist, no primocane or fall-bearing cultivars have been developed. Ironically, primocanes and floricanes are in competition for the energies of the plant, which can affect how each type is grown.

Culture

Pruning, training, and general culture vary somewhat with each type of plant as detailed below.

Red/Yellow Raspberry, *Rubus idaeus*

Plantings can last 10 to 15 years with good care. Red raspberry grows upright canes, which can be grown in a narrow hedgerow or in hills of multiple canes. These spread by shoots arising from the roots, and so they can quickly become too thick to produce optimally. Consequently, canes should be thinned out to the sturdiest few in the hill or to a narrow continuous row of sturdy canes.

Floricane types: These are the ones which grow vegetatively (primocane) in the first season, which then are induced to fruit in the second season as floricanes. This type grows fairly tall and needs some trellising for support. When starting out with a new planting, they are spaced 2 to 3 feet apart in rows 10 feet apart. Remove dying canes immediately after fruiting, if diseases are a problem, or allow them to die completely and remove during late winter pruning if diseases are not a problem. This will allow the plants to fully reabsorb nutrients from the dying canes.

Primocane types: These have been selected for their ability to fruit on the first-year canes, without a chilling requirement to initiate flowering. They begin to flower from the terminal of the shoot and then spiral downward until cold weather terminates growth for the season. The portion which has fruited will die over the winter and is pruned out in late winter or early spring. These canes will resume flowering on the remaining nodes, produce fruit, and then die when all floriferous nodes are depleted. Primocane raspberries are usually grown in hedgerows 1 foot wide, with excess canes removed before fruiting commences in late summer. Since they do not grow as tall as the floricane type, they are sometimes grown without a trellis or other support.

Since primocanes and floricanes compete for the resources of the plant, the first growth of primocanes in a season is sometimes removed or cut back to delay this competition, to allow stronger growth, flowering, and fruit development on the floricanes. For this same reason, the remaining part of the primocanes which fruited in the fall is sometimes removed back to the ground in the spring, to allow new primocanes to develop to their fullest for a greater fall crop. This also may lessen disease pressure which can build up on canes in their second year. Canes in this system may grow taller than those in competition with floricanes, and may need some basic support.

Black Raspberry, *R. occidentalis*
Purple Raspberry, *R.* x *neglectus*

New plantings are usually spaced 2 to 3 feet apart in rows 10 feet apart, using plants from tip rooting or tissue culture. These are the shortest-lived of the brambles and the planting may only last 5 to10 years. Some simple support system is usually used. New canes are generally tipped in summer, back to about 3 feet, to encourage branching. These branches are then pruned back in spring, leaving fewer, stronger buds farther back on the branches to fruit. Dead floricanes are removed during winter pruning. Although primocane bearing has been seen in black raspberries, no available cultivars with this trait have been developed. Since red raspberries can harbor diseases more devastating to black raspberries, the two should not be grown in close proximity.

Although purple raspberries are a cross between red and black types, their growth and reproductive habits are like those of the black raspberry, with long canes which arch down to the ground and tip layer and root at the tips, 6 to 8 feet from the mother plant. These should be pruned and treated like those of black raspberry.

Blackberry, *Rubus* subgenus *Rubus* inter-specific hybrids

Plantings of all growth types may last 1 to 20 years or longer.

Upright

Cultivars of this type produce stiff, upright canes, 4 to 7 feet in length. Upright types produce numerous new shoots from root suckers to form a hedgerow, and canes will probably need to be thinned to lessen competition due to overcrowding. Original plants are set 3 to 4 feet apart in rows 10 feet apart. During the season, primocanes are tipped to encourage branching. After fruit harvest, or in winter, dead floricanes are removed. Primocane branches are usually shortened to 18 inches in late winter. Because of their stiff upright growth habit, this type can be grown without a trellis, in some places, but may have a tendency to break off at ground level in the wind when heavy with fruit. A two- to four-wire trellis system is often used for support and protection. Primocane varieties of this type show promise for future production.

Semi-Upright

These are thornless, grow from a crown, and produce very vigorous erect canes that can grow to 12 to16 feet in length, arching to the ground. Both upright and semi-upright types have similar fruit characteristics, producing fruit which is rounder, firmer, and less aromatic than trailing types. Typical in-row spacing of 4 to 6 feet with 10 feet between rows is common for this type. Primocanes are sometimes summer tipped to encourage branching. Dead floricanes are removed in winter when the branches of primocanes are also shortened. These canes are then trained to a multi-wire trellis.

Trailing Blackberry, *Rubus laciniatus* 'Evergreen', *Rubus laciniatus* 'Thornless Evergreen', and *Rubus laciniatus* 'Everthornless' as well as other interspecific hybrids

Trailing types are crown-forming with very long canes that trail along the ground if not tied to a trellis. Fruit quality is excellent, but winter hardiness is less than other types. They are usually grown with an in-row spacing of 3 to 6 feet, with 10 feet between rows. These can be grown in an every-year system or an alternate-year system. In the every-year system, primocanes are grown along the ground, with the floricanes tied to the wire trellis above. In February, the spent floricanes are removed and the primocanes tied to the wires for fruiting the following season. Remaining at ground level through the worst of winter weather provides a little more winter protection to the primocanes.

In the alternate year system, both the floricanes and the primocanes are removed after fruiting has completed. The following year, the primocanes which sprout and grow are tied to the wires as they grow and then fruit the following year. Again, at the end of the fruiting year, both floricanes and primocanes are removed. Reportedly, yield from this system is 85% of the every year system, due to the increased vigor of the primocanes due to the lack of competition as they are growing.

Close-up of wineberries (*Rubus phoenicolasius*) in various stages of ripening. *Susan Belsinger*

Wineberry (*Rubus phoenicolasius*): A Tasty Invasive

This bramble originates from Japan and eastern Asia, but it was imported for breeding to create new raspberry cultivars. It does make interspecific crosses with both raspberry and blackberry and may have continuing genetic value for this purpose. It has escaped and can now be found growing from southern Georgia west through Tennessee, and northward to the Great Lakes, Canada, and Maine. Both Connecticut and Massachusetts list it as a noxious weed. This would indicate that conscious cultivation of this invasive plant would be irresponsible in other areas of North America. Where it has naturalized, the fruit can be harvested for a sweet treat, however, without encouraging its further invasion.

The entire plant is covered with tiny red hairs and sharp prickles. The compound leaves are made up of three heart-shaped, toothed leaflets. Leaves alternate along the stem and are green on the upper surface and white on the underside. Cane growth habit is most similar to black raspberry, growing to 9 feet in length and arching down to tip layer and form new plants. Immature fruit are encased in a spiny calyx until maturity, when the lobes open up to reveal the little red jewels, which are coated in a sticky substance which may serve as a protectant until full maturity. Although smaller than the average raspberry fruit, when fully ripe, they have a wonderful flavor, sweeter than red raspberry but with a tart undertone.

Given the range above, it would appear that winter hardiness is not an issue with wineberry, though in northeastern Illinois it has borne fruit only 3 times in the 40 years it has been in the author's garden, a gift from a friend in Kentucky where it grew along the edges of a cow pasture. The primocanes have seldom survived to become floricanes the following year in the author's garden. If not a hardiness issue, this might be a disease issue, as they tend to grow entwined with native black raspberries, which might infect them with something deadly to canes but not the roots, which dependably send up new primocanes each year.

Although wineberries are a taste treat, consciously introducing them to new territory is seriously discouraged, notwithstanding the author's innocent folly in 1977. Possibly because they have seldom set seeds, there has been no sign of propagation or invasion, other than creeping forward from their original site, due to tip layering, through all those years. It is better to be lucky than learned sometimes.

References

"Blackberry." *Alternative Nature Online Herbal.* Accessed 8/8/2019. https://altnature.com/gallery/blackberry.htm.

"Blackcap Raspberry: Rubus leucodermis." *Native Plants PNW: An Encyclopedia of the Cultural and Natural History of Northwest Native Plants.* Accessed 8/8/2019. http://nativeplantspnw.com/the-native-plants/.

Crandall, Perry C., PhD. *Bramble Production: The Management and Marketing of Raspberries and Blackberries.* Food Products Press, 1995.

"Dewberry." *Wikipedia.* Accessed 8/8/2019. https://wikipedia.org/wiki/Dewberry.

Frazier, N.W., ed. *Virus Diseases of Small Fruits and Grapevines.* University of California Press, Div of Agricultural Sci, 1970.

"The Genus Rubus." *The Worldwide Fruits.* Accessed 8/8/2019. https://worldwidefruits.com/genus-rubus.html.

"Invasive Plants in Pennsylvania: Wineberry, Rubus phoenicolasius." *Pennsylvania Department of Conservation and Natural Resources.*

Jennings, D. L. *Raspberries and Blackberries: Their Breeding, Diseases and Growth.* Academic Press, 1988.

Martin, Corinne. "Witch Hazel and Blackberry Medicinal Uses." *Mother Earth News,* August/September, 1992.

Martin, Robert R., Michael A. Ellis, Brian Williamson, and Roger N. Williams, eds. *Compendium of Raspberry and Blackberry Diseases,* 2 ed. The American Phytopathological Society. APS Press, 2017.

"Medicinal Uses & Benefits of Raspberry Leaf." Accessed 8/8/2019. www.mountainroseherbs.com/products/raspberry-leaf/profile.

Nagdeve, Meenakshi. "15 Best Blackberry Benefits." *Organic Facts.* Accessed April 25, 2019. /www.organicfacts.net/health-benefits/fruit/blackberries.html.

Patil, Kiran. "Impressive Benefits of Raspberries." *Organic Facts.* Accessed July 24, 2019. www.organicfacts.net/health-benefits/fruit/raspberries.html.

"Raspberry." *Encyclopedia Britannica,* 2019. Accessed 8/15/19. www.britannica.com/search?query=blackberries.

"Red Raspberry, Other Names." *Web MD.* Accessed 8/8/2019. www.webmd.com/vitamins/ai/ingredientmono-309/red-raspberry.

"Rubus flagellaris." *North Carolina Extension Gardener Plant Toolbox.* Accessed 8/9/2019. https://plants.ces.ncsu.edu/plants/rubus-flagellaris/.

"Rubus." *Gardenology.org.* Plant Encyclopedia and Gardening wiki. Accessed 8/8/2019. http://www.gardenology.org/wiki/Rubus.

Smolarz, Kazimierz and Krzysztof Zmarlicki, eds. *Sixth International Symposium on Rubus and Ribes.* International Society for Horticultural Science, Skierniewice, Poland, 1993.

"Species Profile: Rubus (Genus)–Blackberry." *Wikipedia.* Accessed 8/19/19. Wikipedia.org/wiki/Rubus/.

"Thimbleberry, Rubus parviflorus." *Native Plants PNW: An Encyclopedia of the Cultural and Natural History of Northwest Native Plants.* Accessed 8/8/2019. http://nativeplantspnw.com/the-native-plants/.

"Top Ten Health Benefits of Raspberries." *Health Fitness Revolution,* February 19, 2016. https://www.healthfitnessrevolution.com/top-10-health-benefits-of-raspberries/.

Turner, David and Ken Muir. *The Handbook of Soft Fruit Growing.* Croom Helm, 1985.

Wells, Katie. "Red Raspberry Leaf & Benefits (for Pregnancy and More). Accessed 7/30/19. https://wellnessmama.com/5107/raspberry-leaf/.

"Wineberry: The Edible Invasive." *The Infinite Spider,* 7/1/16. Accessed 7/18/19. https://infinitespider.com/wineberry-the-edible-invasive/.

Charles Voigt is a retired faculty member at the University of Illinois at Urbana-Champaign. He was a state vegetable and herb specialist there from 1988 through 2015. In 1989, he was on the steering committee that wrote the bylaws forming the Illinois Herb Association. He first presented a talk at the International Herb Growers and Marketers Association (later renamed International Herb Association or IHA) in 1991. In 2014 in Toronto, he presented the Otto Richter Memorial Lecture at the annual IHA conference. He served on the IHA Program Committee for many years and has been the chair of the Horticulture Committee since 1997 which is instrumental in choosing and promoting Herbs of the Year. Chuck is currently the chair of the IHA Foundation. He also wrote the popular book, *Vegetable Gardening in the Midwest,* with his vegetable mentor, Dr. Joseph Vandemark. One of Chuck's goals in retirement is to sing in 100 gardens.

Just-emerging leaves on wineberry stalk. *Susan Belsinger*

Rubus leaves have traditionally been used alone or combined with other herbs in remedies. Clockwise from left, raspberry leaves, blackberry leaves, lemon balm leaves, chamomile flowers. *Susan Belsinger*

Food and Medicine: Indigenous Peoples' Use of *Rubus*

Kathleen Connole

Rubus species are members of the large family Rosaceae, which contains approximately 122 genera and 3,370 species of trees, shrubs, and herbs. Rosaceae are known worldwide, primarily in northern temperate regions, where they inhabit a wide range of environments on all continents except Antarctica.

Fossil records of the rose family, including *Rubus,* date to as far back as the Eocene Era, 54 to 38 million years ago. The climate during this epoch was warm and rainy, and sea levels were low, exposing the land bridges between Asia and North America via the Bering Strait; North America and Europe via Greenland; and the connection between Australia and Antarctica (*stonerosefossil.org*).

According to *theplantlist.org*, a database compiled by the Royal Botanic Gardens, Kew, and the Missouri Botanical Garden, and a working list of all known plant species, the genus *Rubus* contains 9785 plant name records. Of these, 2208 are scientific plant names of species rank for the genus *Rubus*, and of these, 331 are classified as accepted species names, with a further 546 plant names of infraspecific rank for the genus.

Species native to North America are not always easy to determine, due to complicated taxonomy, multiple synonyms, and the fact that those introduced from elsewhere so readily become naturalized. One example is *Rubus idaeus* L., European raspberry, which Linnaeus named for Mount Ida, Turkey, as it originated in the southern European mountains (*semanticscholar.org*). *R. idaeus* is often also called American raspberry, and the PLANTS database lists it as *both*, meaning that it is considered native and introduced. The Native American Ethnobotany database lists 132 uses for this plant by the native peoples (*naeb.brit.org*).

The PLANTS database is a collaborative effort compiled by the Natural Resources Conservation Service (NRCS), the NRCS Information Technology Center (ITC), and the USDA National Information Technology Center (NITC), and the National Plant Data Team (NPDT). This database contains "standardized information about vascular plants, mosses, liverworts, hornworts, and lichens of North America and all additional U.S. territories and protectorates" (*plants.usda.gov*). It lists several hundred *Rubus* species, many with multiple synonyms, and includes both native and introduced (naturalized) species.

The Native American Ethnobotany Database lists 28 *Rubus* species that were used by the indigenous peoples of North America for food and medicine. This online database, originally created using the research compiled by Daniel E. Moerman in his book *Native American Ethnobotany* (1998), now contains 44,691 items, representing the use of plants for food, medicine, dyes, and fibers by 291 Native American groups, and includes 4,029 species from 243 plant families. The current database lists each additional source of information, with the titles and authors of publications, following the plant's scientific name, the tribe name, and their reported uses. In 2003, links were added to the USDA PLANTS database for access to complete botanical information, pictures, range maps, and endangered status of listed plants.

Since there are numerous species that are known to grow in North America, and because the information on uses by native peoples is very similar for most species, it stands to reason that there could be many more that are not mentioned here, that they were also used for food and medicine, anywhere that they could be found, and by any of the people living in that area.

In order to organize the *Rubus* species into groups according to their uses by certain native peoples, it makes sense to look at the regions where each species originated or grew wild, along with the corresponding peoples who lived in those regions.

Regional cultures of the indigenous peoples of North America, as defined by *The Encyclopedia of Native American Tribes of North America*

Northeast Woodlands: North Atlantic coast, Great Lakes, adjacent southern Canada

This area includes the Atlantic coastal maritime region, the plains area between the Atlantic and the Allegheny and Appalachian Mountains, the fertile Ohio and Mississippi River bottomlands, and the Great Lakes. It contains deciduous and evergreen forests that are home to many large and small mammals, birds, and fish. The people of this region sustained themselves with hunting, fishing, gathering wild plant foods, and limited agriculture, including the cultivation of wild rice.

Tribes or groups known to make their homes here included Chippewa, Delaware, Iroquois, Menominee, Meskwaki, Micmac, Mohegan, Ojibwa, Potawatomi, and Shinnecock.

Rubus species native to this region: *R. allegheniensis* T.C. Porter, sow-teat blackberry; *R. argutus* Link, sawtooth blackberry; *R. canadensis* L., smooth blackberry; *R. chamaemorus* L., cloudberry; *R. cuneifolius* Pursh, sand blackberry; *R. flagellaris* Willd., North American dewberry; *R. frondosus* (Torr.) Bigelow, Yankee blackberry; *R. fruticosus* L., shrubby blackberry; *R. hispidus* L., swamp dewberry; *R. idaeus* subsp. *strigosus* (Michx.) Focke, American red raspberry; *R. occidentalis* L., black raspberry; *R. odoratus* L., purple flowering raspberry; *R. pubescens* Raf., dwarf red blackberry; *R. rosaceus* Weihe, red raspberry.

Southeast Woodlands: South Atlantic coast, Gulf of Mexico, west to the Mississippi River

The southeast woodlands contain mixed broadleaf deciduous and coniferous forests and a very large and diverse population of mammals, birds, fish, reptiles, and amphibians.

The indigenous peoples hunted, fished the rivers and the Atlantic coast, gathered many types of wild plant foods, and grew domesticated crops of various nutritious seeds, followed later by corn, beans, squash, and tobacco.

Rubus species native to this region include *R. allegheniensis*; *R. argutus*; *R. canadensis*; *R. cuneifolius*; *R. frondosus*; *R. hispidus*; *R. ideaus* subsp. *strigosus*; *R. occidentalis*; *R. odoratus*; and *R. trivialis* Michx., southern dewberry.

The groups listed as using *Rubus* in this area include the Cherokee, Seminole, and Rappahannock.

Plains and Prairie: Mississippi River Valley west to the Rocky Mountains, Saskatchewan River in the north to the Rio Grande in the south

The western high plains are very arid short-grass prairie lands. The eastern parts of this area have more precipitation, rich dark soil, and tallgrass prairie lands. Forested patches occur along the Mississippi and Missouri river corridors.

Hunting the abundant large mammals and gathering wild plant foods provided food for the indigenous peoples. Cultivated crops of corn, beans, squash, and sunflowers became an integral part of some groups' diets in later years.

The people inhabiting this area included Cree, Ojibwa, Dakota, Pawnee, Omaha, Ponca, and Shoshone.

Rubus species known to grow in this region that were used by the natives: *R. chamaemorus*; *R. flagellaris*; *R. frondosus*; *R. leucodermis* Dougl. ex Torr. & A. Gray, blackcap raspberry; *R. occidentalis*; *R. parviflorus* Nutt., thimbleberry.

Southwest: New Mexico, Arizona, adjacent parts of Mexico and Texas

The natives of the southwest region hunted small animals, gathered wild plant foods, and raised corn, beans, and squash.

The people listed as having used *Rubus* for food and medicine include Apache, Chiracahua Apache, Mescalero Apache, and Navajo.

Rubus species mentioned that grow in this region: *R. arizonensis* Focke, Arizona dewberry; *R. leucodermis*; *R. parviflorus*.

Plateau: Mountainous area of the northwestern United States, southern British Columbia, Canada

This region contains barren uplands, mountains with areas of forests and lakes, and is home to the Columbia River and its tributary, the Snake River. This region provided abundant protein sources from hunting and fishing and was home to a wide variety of edible plant foods.

The original people of the plateau included Klamath, Salish, Coeur d'Alene,

Spokane, Colville, Okanagan, Thompson, Shuswap, Shoshone, Montana and Karok.

The *Rubus* species listed for this region and that were used by the natives: *R. idaeus* subsp. *strigosus; R. leucodermis*; and *R. parviflorus.*

The Great Basin: Nevada, Utah, Western Colorado, Wyoming, Southern Idaho, and adjacent parts of Oregon and California

This area contains very sparse vegetation and animal resources; subsistence was a daily struggle.

The indigenous peoples inhabiting this area included Shoshone, Paiute, and Gosiute.

Rubus species used in this region include *R. leucodermis* and *R. parviflorus.*

Northwest Coast: Coastal Alaska, British Columbia, Washington, Oregon

Native peoples of this region had many resources. The forests contained many plant foods, fish were plentiful in the rivers, and the Pacific Ocean provided protein and fat from sea mammals.

The indigenous people inhabiting this area included Bella Coola, Squamish, Swinomish, Cowlitz, Puyallup, Quinault, Chimakum, Quileute, Chinook, Hoh, Makah, Carrier, Coast Salish, Okanagan, Shuswap, Squaxon, Haisia, Thompson, Cehalis, Green River Group, Kitasoo, and Klallam.

Rubus that grow wild in this region: R. *idaeus* subsp. *strigosus; R. lasiococcus* Gray, roughfruit berry; *R. leucodermis*; *R. nivalis* Dougl. ex Hook, snow raspberry; *R. parviflorus*; *R. pedatus* Sm., strawberry leaf raspberry; *R. pubescens* Raf., dwarf red raspberry; *R. spectabilis* Pursh, salmonberry; *R. ursinus* Cham. & Schlect, California blackberry; and *R. vitifolius* Cham. & Schlect, Pacific dewberry.

The Mount Pisgah Arboretum, Eugene, Oregon, has information on *R. spectabilis*, and states that "salmonberry patches frequently 'belonged' to a certain family; the owner was the exclusive gatherer until there were enough accumulated for a feast. Then the whole tribe could gather from the patch" (*mountpisgahorboretum.com*).

Petals fall off after fertilization takes place. *Susan Belsinger*

California: Largely, but not entirely, area of present state
(The northern part of California is included in the Northwest Coast culture.)

Small game, wild plants, and limited agriculture sustained the people of this area.

Native peoples of California included Cahuilla, Costanoan, Karok, Pomo, Mendocino, Shoshone, Yuki, Luiseño, Paiute.

Rubus species of California used include *R. leucodermis*; *R. parviflorus*; *R. ursinus*; *R. vitifolius*.

Subarctic, Arctic: Northern interior of Canada, Alaska; northern edge of North America between Alaska and Greenland

Hunting large mammals including those of the sea, fishing the rivers, and gathering wild food plants were the sources of nutrition.

Native people inhabiting this area included Carrier, Northern Ojibwa, Cree, Koyukon, Tanaina, Eskimo (Inuit), Chippewa, Anticosti, and Alaska Native.

Rubus species native to this area: *R. arcticus* L., Arctic raspberry; *R. chamaemorus*; *R. leucodermis*; *R. parviflorus*; *R. pedatus*; and *R. spectabilis*.

Common Indigenous Uses of *Rubus* Species

Many of the ways in which *Rubus* was used by native peoples of North America were common to all species, according to the Native American Ethnobotany Database, *naeb.brit.org*.

Root infusions were used to treat diarrhea, dysentery, stomachache, bowel trouble in children, as a tonic for influenza, rheumatism, cold remedy, febrifuge, emetic, and as an appetite stimulant. A wash of the root infusion was used for hemorrhoids, a coated tongue, and for sore eyes. The root was chewed to ease a cough or toothache.

Root decoctions were used as a blood remedy, for fever, consumption (tuberculosis), colds and coughs, stomach trouble and dysentery, female weakness, gonorrhea, summer complaints, pimples and blackheads, and as an antidote for poison. A poultice of the root was applied to the newborn child's navel to promote healing. The root was also used as a *seasoner* (adjuvant) in other medicines. Root bark was also decocted for diarrhea, dysentery, and

Receptacles remain after picking wineberries or raspberries. *Susan Belsinger*

sore eyes.

The leaves of various *Rubus* species had many uses. They were eaten for internal disorders. An infusion of leaves was used to treat boils, as a dermatological aid, for help with unusually long menses, and as a liver aid to remove bile (emetic). A strong leaf infusion was given to ease childbirth pains.

Leaf decoctions were used as an antihemorrhagic (for spitting or vomiting blood), as an astringent for bowel complaints and a wash for old, foul sores, and for anemia to strengthen blood. Dried leaves were used as a poultice and burn dressing and chewed for stomach ache. The powdered dry leaves were applied to wounds and burns to prevent scarring. Brown leaves were made into tea in the fall.

Rubus plant compounds were also used. One such use listed was as snuff for catarrh (inflammation of the mucous membrane of the nose or throat). A root and lower stem decoction was given to infertile women; to treat coughs, fever, and consumption; and as a measles remedy. Root and leaf infusion was used for diarrhea and rheumatism. *Rubus* root was combined with St. John's Wort (*Hypericum perforatum*) to treat consumption.

A compound decoction was used as a urinary aid, for venereal disease, as an astringent and tonic, for women who had a miscarriage, and as a pulmonary aid. A complex infusion was used for chronic conditions. A decoction of stalks and leaves was considered to be an effective kidney medicine.

Other plant parts were employed medicinally. The canes were used in an infusion or decoction as a diuretic, and to settle the stomach. Berries were infused and used as a vermifuge; juice from the berries was used to treat dysentery and diarrhea; and a fermented decoction of berries was also used for dysentery and as a tonic.

Green insect galls found on stems were burned and the ashes rubbed on a newborn's navel to promote healing. Leaf ash was used with grease as a poultice for swellings.

One puzzling use listed was to "scratch rheumatism" with a thorny branch. According to J. T. Garrett in *The Cherokee Herbal,* "The painful or inflamed area was scratched by the prickly stem of a raspberry plant; then the root (preparation) would be applied to the scratch" (92).

Other interesting uses for *Rubus* were termed *witchcraft*. A decoction was taken by the hunter and his wife to prevent her from fooling around while he was away; it was also given to dogs to make them good hunters and to protect them from theft. Practical uses included placing leaves inside forest runners' shoes to protect their feet. *Rubus* bark was boiled and used as soap while the soft, fuzzy leaves of some *Rubus* species were used as "nature's toilet paper." Berries were used as a dye by some groups.

Rubus leaves were used "to whip soapberries." This refers to the berries of *Shepherdia canadensis* (L.) Nutt., native to the Pacific Northwest. These bitter-tasting berries contain saponin and were eaten by many tribes of the region after whipping them into a froth and adding some type of sweetener, such as salal berries, *Gaultheriea shallon* Pursh, or camas root, *Camassia quamash* (Pursh) Greene, and later, sugar. This dish was called "Indian ice cream."

Rubus served also as both food and beverage. Young shoots in spring were peeled and eaten raw, or fried, steamed, or boiled, or toasted with meat or fish. Young leaves were also eaten as a green. Leaves were made into a tea for a beverage; berries could be made into juice.

Fresh berries—spoken of as "highly esteemed" and a "principle food"—were revered as a delicacy. They were often combined with dried salmon roe. One group ate the berries only to quench thirst.

The berries were an important food source that could be stored for future use in winter. Many groups made them into pulpy cakes which were spread on birch bark and dried, either by the sun or over a fire. The cakes could be stored in a cache and taken as hunting food, or they would be soaked in warm water and cooked as a sauce, pudding, porridge, or soup; or mixed with cornbread.

The far northern groups also froze the berries and stored them in caches. These groups often mixed them with seal oil or caribou tallow; with sugar added, this became a sort of ice cream. Once sugar became available, the berries were made into jams, jellies, and pies.

Rubus leaves had other culinary uses. Leaves were boiled with fish as flavoring and to keep it from sticking to the pot; they were placed above and below seaweed in steaming pots and used to wrap meat and other food for baking. Leaves were also used to wrap cooked elderberries; as storage containers; to line berry baskets and between layers of fresh berries; to dry

Ronce odorante (*Rubus odoratus*).
Jardin Botanique, Montreal, Canada. *Gert Coleman*

berries on; and to wipe the slime from salmon.

J.T. Garrett, a member of the Eastern Band of the Cherokee from North Carolina, writes of the Medicine Way taught to him by his elders. He stresses the importance of having respect for the elders and their knowledge passed down through the generations. He also expresses appreciation for "the travelers" like William Bartram, realizing that these botanists and naturalists have helped to preserve a valuable resource in their writings about the plants that they encountered in their travels in early America.

The Cherokee people of eastern North America also felt a sense of kinship with the people of European descent who settled in their homeland, calling them "mountain folks" and "friends of the Cherokee." Garrett says that "these were hardy people respected by the tribes for their values and for the willingness to live in harmonious cohabitation with the environment" (3).

The philosophy of Mr. Garrett is well worth remembering: "Healing was not based on a treatment; it was based on a way of bringing a person into harmony and balance with their environment….From a Cherokee perspective it was important to understand the relations of plants as helpers in bringing the circle into harmony and balance….The humans share the world with plants, which act as phytomedicines to sustain life" (22).

When I was a child, my siblings and cousins knew of an unspoken family legend that our grandfather, my mother's father, had Native American ancestry. We dared not ask him to speak of it, as when he grew up in the early 1900s, this was not something to be proud of. Every summer my mother would take Grandfather and us kids for a ride out into the backwoods of the southeastern Missouri Ozarks, to a little homestead with hill folks and their many critters. We traipsed through the woods there until he came to a large flat rock with ancient symbols and writing. This we would look at in amazement, then pile into the car, and take him back home. Our mother also took us on many spring wildflower walks in the woods where Granny and Grandfather made their home.

My brother and sisters and I have always felt a special connection to nature, and a need to experience wild places. In fact, that would be why I ended up in the hills of Arkansas, to "reinvent" my life, in 2005. All these many years later, a friend of the family decided to research our family tree and now we have an actual photograph of my grandfather's grandmother, and she was indeed Cherokee. How I wish now that I would have paid more attention to the stories of our elders!

References

"Accepted scientific names of species rank for genus Rubus." Accessed 5/21/19. www.theplantlist.org.

Bailey, L.H. *Hortorium of Cornell University. Hortus Third: A Concise Dictionary of Plants Cultivated in the United States and Canada.* Macmillan,1976.

Barnes, Dr. Jan. *The Historical Atlas of Native Americans.* Chartwell Books, Inc., 2010.

Ethnobotanical information on Rubus species." Accessed 7/7/19. www.naeb.brit.org.

Fagan, Brian. *The First North Americans.* Thames & Hudson Ltd, 2011.

"Fossil History of Rosaceae." Accessed 5/23/19. www.stonerosefossil.org.

Garrett, J.T. *The Cherokee Herbal.* Bear & Co., 2003.

Johnson, M.G. and R. Hook. *Encyclopedia of Native Tribes of North America.* Compendium Publishing Limited, 2007.

"List of Rubus species, maps of distribution." Accessed 6/14/19. www.plants.usda.gov.

Moerman, Daniel E. *Native American Medicinal Plants.* Timber Press, 2009.

"Rubus ideaus L. var. strigosus (Mich.) Focke." Accessed 7/7/19. www. pfaf.org.

"Rubus Pharmacology: Antiquity to Present." Accessed 5/ 22/19. www.semanticscholar.org

---

Kathleen Connole is a native of the Missouri Ozarks, where she and her family spent many hours exploring the natural wonders of the St. Francois Mountains. She attended the University of Missouri–Columbia, where she met her future husband and Kansas City, Missouri, native Jeffrey. After raising three children, Kathleen resumed her college education and earned a Bachelor of Science in Plant Science. Her horticultural experiences include internships at Powell Gardens, and a stint as a greenhouse grower and container garden designer at Farrand Farms, one of Kansas City's premier garden centers. In 2005 Kathleen and Jeffrey uprooted and moved to Buffalo River Country in Arkansas. Kathleen became a student in Tina Marie Wilcox's Ozark Folk School class, in the spring of 2006. Several months later she joined the Ozark Folk Center's Heritage Herb Garden team. Kathleen serves as chair of the Herb Society of America Ozark Unit. This group holds monthly meetings at the Ozark Folk Center State Park, takes an active role in the herbal events hosted there, and helps maintain the Folk Kids' Mountain Garden. Kathleen serves on the International Herb Association's board of directors.

Knowing Rubus

Wild brambles arching above California coast at Mendocino. *Bonny Lundy*

Product of Mexico
Hank Kalet

Rubus armeniacus
is considered
an invasive species, a weed
spreading wild, brambling along
the river banks. But under
a dusky, Mexican sky, the Tupi
blackberry, stretches out
far from its roots. Drupelets pop
in aggregation, darken. And the pickers
come and pinch the stems,
pile blackberries
in plastic pails, as thrashers
circle, dive, pick
what they can steal.

I did a story once
on a pick-your-own farm, pricked
my fingers, tore my shirt as I
flailed against the swarm
of bees in the thorny bush.

In the fields, men sweated
over the green leaves of spinach,
using small knives to clean
the stalk. Come July,
when the families ceased their
recreational harvest, the men,

speaking Spanish, would throw
themselves into the berry brush, whack
away at the rotting berries
and cut it all back until
the new season bloomed.

Now, almost thirty years later,
berries cross the border
in a wave. Blackberries. Raspberries.
Blueberries. Cartons and clam-shell
plastic containers loaded
with berries line the supermarket
cold case. Buy one, get one.
Product of Mexico. Guatemala.
Points farther south. Five pounds
a year we eat, the paper said.
And the pickers make twenty bucks
a day until their fingers bleed.

Hank Kalet is a poet, journalist and editor. His journalism appears regularly in *NJ Spotlight* and *The Progressive Populist.* His most recent book, *As an Alien in a Land of Promise,* is a hybrid work of poetry that uses the methods of journalism to tell the story of a homeless encampment in Lakewood, New Jersey. He lives in South Brunswick, NJ, with his wife Annie and two dogs, Rosie and Sophie. An adjunct professor of English at Middlesex County College, he is also a part-time lecturer in journalism at Rutgers University. hankkalet@gmail.com

Blackberry Magic: A Game of Thorns

Gert Coleman

*If a plant has thorns, it is probably edible
and evolved the thorns to protect itself.*
Ellen Evert Hoffman, Secret Medicines from Your Garden.

Common Names for Blackberry: Blackberry, Asian Blackberry, Black Long Berry, Blegs, Bumble-kite, Blackbrides, Black-boyds, Black Spice, Black-bowours, Bly, Bramble, Bramble Apple, Brambleberry, Brameberry, Brombeere, Brummel, Bummel-berries, Bummel-kites, Cloud Berry, Dewberry, Doctor's Medicine, Fingerberry, Gatter Berry, Gout Berry, High Blackberry, Himalayan Blackberry, Mushes, Thimbleberry, Ronce, Sméara Dubha, Scald-head

Watch out for the thorns! Ouch!

I've spent a lot of time among the blackberries (*Rubus fruticosus*) lately. Luminous spring flowers give way to dark juicy berries in summer, then deep red leaves in the fall. But, always, there are thorns. These memorable thorns, so popular in fairy tales for marking boundaries, wounding heroes, and keeping out the world, have long been used in magic and medicine for protection, prosperity, and healing.

In getting to know the actual plant, the first thing you learn is, Respect the Thorns.

Make no mistake: blackberry's recurved thorns can inflict pain and suffering. The canes catch at arms, torso, and hair, but we can learn to avoid and minimize damage, a good skill for negotiating relationships of all kinds. Researching "Thorn Medicine" turns up numerous sites detailing the careful extraction of embedded thorns without further damage or infection. Interestingly, a strong blackberry leaf infusion can be patted on the wound to ease the discomfort. Even easier, crushed fresh leaves offer a styptic effect on wounds, stopping bleeding, a perfect emergency remedy in the blackberry thicket.

Prized for its sweet ripe fruit, healing qualities, and hedgerow growing patterns, the beloved blackberry is magical in many ways that may not be immediately obvious to contemporary readers. The ancients inferred a plant's *magic*—what we now think of as science—from its properties and setting. Herbs appeal to all senses, and the magical powers in herbs can be determined by the plant's habitat, scent, color, form, and other aspects. As used here, the term *magic* reflects the medicinal, religious, folkloric, and culinary practices of a culture.

Available year-round in today's supermarkets, fresh or frozen blackberries add flavor and fiber to any meal, from oatmeal to salads to fish and fowl as well as a host of tantalizing desserts and beverages. In previous centuries, folks spent summers *brambling*, that is, braving the tangles of thorns to harvest and preserve blackberries for winter. To go brambling meant knowing where the wild berries grew, on whose property, and whether it would be allowed. Blackberry thorns teach us to respect and establish boundaries.

Blackberry fruits were eaten fresh, infused into syrups and cordials, and dried on nets and cloths for winter use. The leaves were gathered carefully—they have prickles, too!—and the astringent roots and canes were cut and dried to cure gout, dysentery, colds, and a host of ailments. So plentiful in the wild, blackberries were not cultivated in farms or gardens until the nineteenth century. Economically, *R. fruticosus* constitutes one of the most valuable wild fruit crops today in North America. Magically, blackberries signify abundance.

Historically, in a display of territoriality and good citizenship, blackberry canes were fashioned into hedgerows to maintain borders. Brambles have a distinctive growth form: long, arching canes—typically erect but some species sprawl—that do not flower until the second year. *Recurved* means to curve or bend (something) back or down or (of something) to be so curved or bent. While there are scores of blackberry microspecies, most have recurved thorns that dig into and tear at skin, hair, and clothes. These daunting thickets deterred invaders while providing shelter to animals and seasonal food and medicine to the citizenry.

Neolithic farmers utilized hedgerows to safeguard crops and animals from predators. Bronze Age and Iron Age peoples made walls, shored up with earth and stone bases, of living plants, especially those with thorns, spines, and prickles, as their version of contemporary barbed wire. Blackberry hedgerows have marked European property lines for millennia. Brehon Law in ancient Ireland recognized the sturdy hedgerow, or living fence, as an official boundary marker. It was illegal to cut them without authorization.

For natural defenses, thorny, invasive plants like blackberry, wild rose, and hawthorn create inexpensive boundaries with medicinal and culinary value. Such plants thrive along embankments and roadsides, the edges of woods, fields, and communal paths, and in waste lots. Irish farmers still cultivate blackberry hedges to protect crops, establish borders, and gather food and medicine.

In rural Europe, hedge cutters were highly regarded for their skills, and kingdoms were judged by their border maintenance. If neglected, a blackberry patch or hedgerow can become an impenetrable thicket with up to five hundred canes per square yard, but with decreased berry production. According to Robert K. Henderson, "Normandy's hedgerows halted tanks in their tracks during World War II." Blackberry makes a formidable living fence.

Anglo-Saxon *braemel*, from *brom*, means broom. Think of the *besom*, or old-fashioned "witch's broom." Thorny blackberry branches were once bunched together and tied to a stout stick or pole to sweep out porches, homes, barns, and driveways. Sweeping one's property is an act of territoriality, keeping one's side of the street clean. Brooms are also used to banish spirits, insects, and unwanted visitors of any kind.

Sturdy blackberry symbolizes resilience, inspiring strength and courage in daunting circumstances. This tenacious plant takes hold in disturbed or untended habitats, healing damaged ground and providing food and shelter for wildlife where there might otherwise be none. This helps to conserve wildlife habitat, an ever-decreasing resource in the face of ongoing global urbanization, and support biodiversity within small eco-zones.

Blackberry's thorny thickets sustain deer, rabbits, reptiles, and rodents, attract bees and butterflies, and provide nesting habitat for catbirds, mockingbirds, robins, sparrows, thrashers, thrushes, turkeys, warblers, wrens, and other birds. According to Staten Island bird expert Howie Fischer, "Gray Catbird, Brown Thrasher, Wood Thrush, and American Robins feed the berries to nestlings and the plants themselves are protective vegetation for many nesting songbirds. Yellow-breasted Chats require dense thickets that provide cover and energy. In cool summers when insects aren't always available for nestlings, adults will feed more fruit to young nestlings. The fruits are a high source of energy given the sugar content; the downside is less protein for developing young birds." In city parks and college campuses, Grey Catbirds depend on the vibrant, red-thorned Wineberry (*R. phoenicolasius*), an attractive invasive with bright red berries.

Thorns remind us of how we handle ourselves in uncomfortable situations. Spending time in *Rubus* patches is a good way to learn about thorns, boundaries, concealment, and effective strategies for disentanglement. Harvesting berries, canes, roots, and leaves, we learn to wear sturdy leather gloves and long sleeves. One blackberry-picking e-group asserts that wearing welding gloves is the way to go. "Not a single thorn came through!"

Wild blackberry offers appealing color in all seasons: pretty white or pink flowers and deep purple fruits against dark green leaves that give way to vivid orange-red-purple in fall and winter. Some Northwest Native American tribes preferred the scarlet leaves to the green as more flavorful in teas. The leaf colors burn so brightly that it's quite easy to see how blackberry was considered the Burning Bush through which God spoke to Moses. Those leaves can hold color through early to mid-winter, depending on arctic blasts.

While my wild blackberries finish in mid-August here in Central New York, elsewhere bushes bear berries into fall. According to English folklore, however, brambling should end before St. Michael's Day, or *Michaelmas* (currently September 29 but October 11 in older calendars). When St. Michael the Archangel threw Lucifer, once the brightest of all angels, out of heaven, he landed ignominiously in a bramble patch. As a result, he annually spits or urinates on the berries on that day, just to be spiteful. A kitten born on Michaelmas Day is called a "Blackberry cat" and is believed to be mischievous all its life

Bramble's speedy ability to turn a hedgerow into an impenetrable forest of menacing thorns is a recurring motif in fairytales. Cursed by a witch, Sleeping Beauty and her kingdom are sequestered by a quick-growing bramble forest. While the Disney movie depicts the prince and his indomitable horse dramatically slashing their way through thorns with nary a scratch, Andrew Lang's version offers a magical entrance to the enchanted kingdom: "Scarce had he advanced towards the wood when all the great trees, the bushes, and brambles gave way of themselves to let him pass through." He faces challenges within the castle, of course, but "a young and amorous prince is always valiant" (*Blue Fairy Book* 58).

In a different fairy tale, another amorous prince tries to rescue Rapunzel from imprisonment in a tower. Tricked by a wicked witch, however, he falls into a patch of thorns, putting his eyes out. He wanders for many years, alone, blind and miserable, eating only roots and berries. At long last he meets Rapunzel

Blackberry bushes offer fall color. *Peter Coleman*

in the desert. Her tears restore his vision and they live happily after.

In a humorous vein, the wily Brer Rabbit in Uncle Remus' tale, caught in a sticky situation, manipulates Brer Fox into thinking that throwing him into a bramble patch is the thing he fears the most. "Skin me, Brer Fox, snatch out my eyeballs, tear out my ears by the roots, and cut off my legs," said Brer Rabbit. "Only please, Brer Fox, please don't throw me into the briar patch." Once Brer Rabbit lands in the thorny briar patch, however, he is home free.

"Born and bred in the briar patch, that's me," laughed Brer Rabbit. "I told you not to throw me there. In all the world, that's the place I love best!" In folk tales, *briar* and *brambles* are often used synonymously.

While quite protective, blackberry nurtures with its abundant, edible fruit, astringent leaves and roots, demonstrating that fierceness and kindness make powerful magic and medicine. Folklore suggests that blackberries, gathered at certain moon phases, protect us from evil, but all parts of the plant have been used. Scottish Highlanders made wreaths of the canes to ward off evil and planted blackberries throughout graveyards to repel evil or wandering spirits. In the home, the less prickly brambles (*R. idaeus*) were sometimes hung at windows and doors after a death to keep the departed spirit from re-entering the house (Cunningham 186).

In Gaelic, blackberry was known as *an druise bennaichte* or "the blessed bramble," alluding to the bramble switch that Jesus used to drive money-changers out of the temple. The crown of thorns forced on Jesus during the Crucifixion ordeal may have been made of blackberry thorns.

Fairies allegedly love blackberry thickets because they keep humans away from their hidden enclaves and boats. Fairies feared human encroachment as much as humans feared fairy ensorcellment. Herbal folklore and poetry are full of examples. William Butler Yeats' poem "The Stolen Child" displays this eerie distrust:

> Where dips the rocky headland
> Of Sleuth Wood in the lake,
> There lies a leafy island
> Where flapping herons wake
> The drowsy water-rats;
> There we've hid our faery vats,
> Full of berries
> And of reddest stolen cherries.
> *Come, away, Oh human child!*
> *To the waters and the wild*
> *With a faery, hand in hand,*
> *For the world's more full of weeping*
> *than you can understand.*

For centuries, blackberry has been used in rituals for healing, protection, and prosperity, especially when the need for funds arises suddenly. Fresh or dried, blackberry roots are useful in spells for locating or improving food and shelter while the leaves aid in spells for expanding business or creative efforts in art and architecture, or when success is related to how we reach out and connect with the world.

Magical lore suggests that adding just one thorn to the berries when making blackberry vinegar, tincture, cordial, or shrub can help shield you from physical and emotional troubles, especially regarding boundaries. Just be sure to strain it out later with the berries! Blackberry vinegar tastes magically delicious, mixes well with water to quench thirst, eases colds, flu, fever, and diarrhea, and reduces the conditions that cause gout to flare up. Both internally and externally, it has been used for arthritis pain. Blackberry syrup has similar restorative powers and some folks spread blackberry jelly on wounds and sprains.

Thorns can be added to amulets and mojo bags to offer protection and help one establish boundaries in life and relationships, alone or in combination with bay leaves and elder twigs. Thorns can be carefully pricked off canes or scraped into a lined basket. Or you can use the leaves for thorn magic. Strongly associated with Brigid, Celtic goddess of the forge and the holy well, blackberry leaves have sharp little spines on the underside along the center vein. These mini-thorns will aid in protective medicine but can also abrade or irritate unprotected skin, creating a burning sensation.

In Cornwall, blackberry leaves were used to treat burns and scalds. To heal burns, one would dip nine blackberry leaves in spring water or holy water and lay them on the wound while saying three times for each leaf,

> *Three ladies come from the east,*
> *One with fire, two with frost.*
> *Out with fire, in with frost.*

To lift enchantments, the Anglo-Saxons combined dried blackberries with the power of numbers and religious beliefs: "Take Bramble Apple, pound and sift them, put them in a pouch, lay them under the altar and sing nine Masses over them. Then put this dust into milk, drip Holy Water three times upon it and drink every three hours." Another version used ten herbs, including bramble, pounded together then boiled in butter. The resulting broth was strained through a special cloth and set under a church altar for nine Masses to be sung over it. In a city church, this could be accomplished in a few days; in smaller, more rural churches, this might take weeks. The blessed salve was then smeared on "a man full of elfin tricks" (Silverman 16).

Ruled by Mars, blackberry reminds us of the daily wars we wage, the hidden dangers, the unraveling of wrongs. To dream of blackberries helps make sense of our fears. Blackberries can mean loss or sorrow, while dreaming of being pricked by blackberry thorns might portend that enemies or trusted friends are conspiring against you. If the thorn draws blood, you can expect serious business reverses. On a positive note, if you pass through the bramble patch unscathed, you will defeat your foes.

Long appreciated for its sweet fruit and healing qualities, blackberry medicine is generally mild and pleasant–tasting, useful for babies of all ages. It is hard to overestimate the faith that folks all over the world have had in this versatile plant.

The Ancient Greeks used both berries and flowers for venomous bites. Globally, dried or green leaves have been infused into mouthwashes and gargles for canker sores, bleeding gums, and sore throats, or used as a wash for genital irritations and skin ulcers taking too long to heal. Leaves and roots were decocted for stomach upsets, dysentery, and women's hormonal ailments, from menses through menopause. According to the Leech Book of Bald (circa 900 AD), fresh leaves were pounded and laid over the chest for heartaches, both physical and emotional. Tudor herbalists mixed blackberry juice with wine and honey to increase "the passions of the heart." Several Native American cultures treated joint pain with blackberry leaf tea. Blackberry juice mixed with honey and lemon is a traditional European cold remedy. Blackberries, sometimes mixed with elderberries, have traditionally been added to wines for deeper color and flavor.

Wild blackberry's vigorous growing habits signal the plant's affinity for women while its bountiful fruit and seeds offer hope for fertility and a safe, easy childbirth. Rural families kept a supply of dried blackberry leaves and roots and preserved the fruits in jams, syrups, cordials, and other beverages. The Pennsylvania Dutch used the leaves, roots, and fruit to treat digestive ailments. Traditional Chinese Medicine (TCM) uses the blackberries to increase virility and body strength. Eating the fresh shoots in spring supposedly tightened loose teeth while preparations of young shoots were used to improve the complexion and to treat fevers and colds. Even the hard-shelled seeds have been crushed for use in skin and hair products. As recently as 1955, the US Dispensatory listed a blackberry extract for health issues.

Blackberry species develop into thickets by rooting at the tips by means of curved thorns which hook onto themselves and neighboring foliage. They require moisture-retentive, humus-rich soil, but are otherwise undemanding, growing well in both full sun and semi-shade. Much magic has been attributed to wild blackberry's arching canes. An arch of bramble which had rooted at both ends was believed to have special healing powers, more so if this occurred at the intersection of adjoining properties.

According to Maude Grieves, "Creeping under a Bramble-bush was itself a charm against rheumatism, boils, blackheads, and other skin ailments." She also cites the time-honored practice of children afflicted with hernias being passed backwards and forwards through the arching bramble. Ancient medicinal practices often included passing sick children through holes in the earth, rocks, and trees, so choosing arched bramble canes isn't as odd as it might first seem.

In addition, young children with whooping cough, bronchial ailments, and skin complaints were made to crawl backwards and forwards three times, from east to west, or, if too ill, were passed by gentle hands through a blackberry arch. Doing this for nine consecutive days was supposed to cure the child, especially if the following was chanted,

> *In bramble,*
> *Out cough,*
> *Here I leave the whooping cough.*

Folks also dragged weak or paralyzed cattle through arched canes, though some may have simply waved the canes over them. An accompanying Irish superstition revealed that finding a piece of bramble attached to a cow's tail was cause for alarm: someone was trying to put a spell on the cow's milk. On a different level, a person might crawl through the arch at Samhain to invoke evil spirits all the while envisioning intent.

Blackberry fruits ripen from green to red to purple-black, representing the Triple Goddess in some beliefs. Both blackberry flowers—whose beauty has been celebrated in Irish ballads—and the fruits can be used as offerings or altar decorations. The celebrated wild fruit of summer, blackberry pies were served on the Celtic feast of Lughnasadh (Loo-nah-sah), later renamed by Lammas or Loaf Mass by Christians, in gratitude for the bounty of the season.

Similarly, Native American tribes served blackberries mixed with honey as ceremonial food, and honored *Rubus* with its own special ceremony. At the first harvest, leaders would ask the spirit of the fruit for help in matters of peace and war. Boundaries again! Any blackberry libation will make a fitting ritual drink for celebrating the autumn equinox.

Universally, humans have relied on *Rubus* varieties for protection, abundance, and medicine for all sorts of ailments. Blackberry's many attributes manifest its "magic" as an herb versatile enough to be included in healing gardens, kitchen gardens, dye gardens, women's gardens, children's gardens, literary gardens, saints' gardens, Biblical and green witch gardens, to name but a few.

Thorny wild blackberries offer color, beauty, food, shelter, and medicine for every season but thornless cultivars are also available for your garden. Deni Bown recommends 'Merton Thornless' and nurseries stock many other varieties. It may make gardening pain-free, but you will deprive yourself of the game of thorns.

> *In memory of Thorne-dog,*
> *Much loved and much missed*

References

Angier, Bradford. *Feasting Free on Wild Edibles.* Stackpole Books, 1973. 37.

"Blackberry." *Witchipedia.* Accessed 10/24/19. www.witchipedia.com/herb:blackberry

Bean, Geneve. "Blackberry." *The Herb Hound,* March 16, 2003. Accessed 11/5/19. https://theherbhound.blogspot.com/2013/03/blackberries-known-also-as-bramble.html.

"Bramble/Blackberry." Accessed 10/24/19. http://irishhedgerows.weebly.com/flora.html.

Bown, Deni. *Herbal: The Essential Guide to Herbs for Living.* Barnes & Noble, Inc. 2001. 231-234.

"Brer Fox, Brer Rabbit and the Briar Patch." Accessed 11/14/19. www.abelard.org/brer_fox_brer_rabbit_briar_patch.php.

Cunningfolk, Alexis J. "The Magick of Thorns." Accessed 10/25/19. www.wortsandcunning.com/blog/the-magick-of-thorns.

Cunningham, Scott. *Cunningham's Encyclopedia of Magical Herbs,* 18 ed. Llewellyn, 1994. 55-56

Dugan, Ellen. *Garden Witch's Herbal.* Llewellyn, 2009. 101-102.

Fernald and Kinsey. *Edible Wild Plants of North America.* Dover, 1958.

Fischer, Howie. Staten Island birding expert. Personal email. 11/11/19.

"Folklore of the Hedgerow." Accessed 10/25/19. http://irishhedgerows.weebly.com/flora.html.

Grieves, Maude. *A Modern Herbal* (1931). Barnes and Noble, 1996. 108-110.

Hagen, Cliff. Staten Island birding expert. Personal email. 11/10/19.

Hoffman, Ellen Evert. *Secret Medicines from Your Garden.* Healing Arts Press, 2016

Henderson, Robert K. "Briar Patch Medicine." Accessed 10/26/19. www.motherearthliving.com/plant-profile/briar-patch-medicine.

Hummer, Kim E. and Jules Janick. "Rubus Iconography: Antiquity to the Renaissance." Accessed 10/25/19. www.hort.purdue.edu/newcrop/rubusicon.pdf.

Hutchens, Alma. *A Handbook of Native American Herbs.* Shambala, 1992.

"Magic of Blackberry, The." Accessed 10/25/19. www.hagstonepublishing.com/single-post/2019/03/13.

Mason. Andy. Co-president, Delaware-Otsego chapter, National Audubon Society. Personal email. 11/10/19.

McDonald, Jim. "Thoughts on thorns." Accessed 10/25/19. www.herbcraft.org/thorns.html.

Needham, William. "Hiker's Notebook: Blackberry." Accessed 10/30/19. www.hikersnotebook.blog/flora/berry-plants-and-fruit-trees/blackberry.

Perryman, Sue. "The Magic of Blackberry." Accessed 10/25/19. www.kitchenwitchhearth.net/post/the-magic-of-blackberry-by-sue-perryman.

"Rapunzel." *The Red Fairy Book.* Andrew Lang, ed. Dover, 1966 (1890).

Scott, Timothy Lee. *Invasive Plant Medicine.* Healing Arts Press, 2010. 196-200.

Silverman, Maida. *A City Herbal.* Knopf, 1977. 12-19.

"Sleeping Beauty in the Wood, The." *The Blue Fairy Book.* Andrew Lang, ed. Dover, 1965 (1889).

Tedesco, Patricia. *A Witch's Brew.* Llewellen, 1995.

Arching canes of wild brambles in midsummer. *Susan Belsinger*

Herb enthusiast **Gert Coleman** loves, grows, eats, and reads avidly about herbs. Retired Professor of English at Middlesex County College in New Jersey and past president of the Staten Island Herb Society, she now lives in Middlefield, New York, where she and her husband are fixing up another old house and planting herbs, flowers, trees, and at-risk native plants. She currently edits the IHA Herb of the Year™ books (*Cilantro & Coriander; Hops: Brewing and Beyond; Agastache: Anise Hyssop, Hummingbird Mint and More!;* and *Rubus*), and frequently writes and teaches about the legends, lore, and poetry of herbs. Gert.coleman@verizon.net

Thimbleberry flowers. *Davy Dabney*

Chasing the Wild Thimbleberry: *Rubus parviflorus*

Davy Dabney

For many years my daughter was director of a senior citizen's center in Sugar Grove, a quaint, rural community in western North Carolina. During my many visits there, I spent as much time as I could talking to the locals who attended each day. At that time, most of the regulars lived within a twenty-mile radius, in places they had lived all their lives. It was amazing how many of them had never met until they came to the center! Most were over 70 years old and had never left the county.

I was intrigued by their stories about life in those remote areas. They were self-sufficient and lived off the land enjoying a simple lifestyle with limited financial resources, yet they never lacked anything, even during economic depressions. Using and selling native herbs was an important part of their daily survival. They foraged and sold or traded wild medicinal plants to local drug companies as their main livelihood. Harvests were abundant. They called the plants by their local names, some of which caused me some confusion. Fortunately, I recognized most of them.

However, there was one plant which grew abundantly in the edges of roadsides and along banks of streams. When asked what it was, they said "thimbleberry." They said they called it that because the flat head of the unripe berry reminded them of the top of a silver thimble. That still didn't make it any easier for me to find what it was. I took several pictures to help me identify it. I soon located it at a locally owned plant nursery called Gardens of the Blue Ridge. All members of the family were very knowledgeable of the local names as well as the proper Latin names. And thimbleberry turned out to be *Rubus parviflorus*.

I was surprised because the large 3-lobed leaves didn't resemble those of any raspberry bushes I'd ever seen. Thimbleberry is a shrub that can grow up to 8 feet tall and 6 feet wide. The plants are vigorous and can be used a barrier or ground cover. The inconspicuous, dusty pale white or pale pink blossoms on woody, thornless canes produce flat berries nestled into small 2-pronged upright-facing leaves. As they ripen, their color changes to a more orange color. They reseed in the fall, or grow from root runners, and may be propagated by root cuttings in the fall. The large 3-lobed leaves are greener than those of other more commonly known raspberries.

At one time the plants were so abundant they provided winter shelter and enough food for birds, animals, and people. They may retain most of their leaves if the winter is not too bitter. The plants have become scarce as roadsides have been ploughed and reseeded with ornamental flowers.

My daughter acquired several thimbleberry canes years ago which have grown into a thick, green hedge edging a portion of her property. Useful in many ways, this hedgerow stops erosion on steep banks. The fragrant flowers attract bees, butterflies, and hummingbirds. They make pretty pressed flowers. The berries are not very juicy but they may be made into jams. Locals use them for medicinal purposes. The astringent leaves are used in the treatment of stomach troubles, a wash for sores, and as a gargle or mouthwash. Tea made from the roots is used to treat colds. A purple, blue, or pale pink dye may be obtained from the berries, depending on which mordant is used.

Recently more people who have moved into the area are recognizing the benefits of using more native plants in their landscaping, so the thimbleberry is regaining its popularity.

Davy Dabney, a founding member of the IHA (originally known as IHGMA, the International Herb Growers and Marketers Association), has been a business owner, an instructor, and mentor in the world of herbs and plants. She is a Life Member of the Herb Society of America, member of the Kentucky Herb Business Association, and owner of Dabney Herbs. With the help of the Wednesday Weeders, she planted and tended a superior herb garden at Farmington Historic Home in Kentucky. From 2003 to 2016, she was Superintendent of the Plant and Flower Department of the Kentucky State Fair, overseeing displays of over 3000 entries including plants and arrangements. She loves learning about exciting new plants, consulting and writing, and sitting on her deck with friends, enjoying the beauty of nature, and letting someone else do the weeding!

Thimbleberry thicket. Note the large three-lobed leaves. *Davy Dabney*

Wasps and beetle on wild blackberries down a dirt road, Arkansas.
Susan Belsinger

Rubus and Shakers of the Herbal World

Skye Suter

Do all your work as if you had a thousand years to live, and as you would if you knew you must die tomorrow.
Testimonies of the Life, Character, Revelations and Doctrines of Our Ever Blessed Mother Ann Lee. Hancock, Massachusetts, 1810

Who are the Shakers?

The Shakers have historically been recognized for their craftsmanship and association with herbs, including *Rubus* roots, leaves, and berries. Blackberries, raspberries, and black raspberries were specifically relevant herbs in their repertoire. Much reference is made to recipes and products made from, or containing blackberries and raspberries for medicinal and culinary purposes. The Shakers were well known for producing and distributing herbs, herbal products, and seeds on a large scale and Shaker medicinal gardens were considered the best in the United States. In their heyday, they could be considered the "movers and shakers" of the herb industry.

Although Shaker communities were already growing and processing herbs at multiple locations, the movement for large scale distribution began at the parent order located in New Lebanon, New York. The demand for Shaker herbs was at its highest point throughout the 1800s and Shaker communities remained the largest source for herbal products and remedies throughout the United States and in Europe at this time.

Other noteworthy communities in the Eastern United States conducting large-scale operations included Watervliet in New York, Enfield and Canterbury in New Hampshire, Harvard and Hancock in Massachusetts, Enfield in

Connecticut, and New Glouster in Maine. Communities in more westerly regions with large-scale production operations included Union Village in Ohio as well as locations in Kentucky and Indiana. Communities in the various states developed herb industries simultaneously to the work going on at the mother, or flagship, community at New Lebanon.

Work Ethic

Work ethic and perseverance made "variety of labor" a source of pleasure and a means of improving time and talent. A Shaker elder once wrote "that members of a community should be willing to turn a hand in any needed direction in order to render their best service in building up and sustaining the cause." A variety of labor might include anything from edging a garden border, creating a cupboard, taking care of a sick brother or sister to helping to raising a building. Certainly, cutting *Rubus* canes and harvesting and drying *Rubus* berries made for a variety of labor.

The holistic Shaker philosophy enabled the communities to turn herbs into a very lucrative business. They approached all aspects of the business with the same meticulous precision, care, and forward vision that was given to their whole way of life. The Shaker approach to the business of herbs welcomed scientific methods and progressive innovations (as in machinery) to cultivate and harvest their herbs. By paying attention to the proper season for cultivating and collecting as well as innovative methods of preparation, they were able to maximize their output to a phenomenal extent.

Shops were created at the communities to sell herbs and herbal products but most of the building space was given to warehousing and production of herbs for distribution throughout the United States and Europe. The Shakers designed buildings and rooms specifically for drying, sorting, storing, or generating extracts, creating powders, and other products. The Shakers were not averse to modern technology, and machinery like distillers, presses, and grinders were often used in production buildings.

Within preparation rooms one could also find thoughtfully planned out and well-constructed drying cupboards, cases, seed drawers, and tools to further the herb business at hand. The Shakers always planned things out carefully and many of their innovations hold up to this day, including garden and seed catalogues, standard-sized seed drawers, and the packets to hold seeds.

Collecting, Growing, Cultivating, Harvesting, Preserving

World famous Shaker gardens yielded a lot of product but astonishing amounts of wild-gathered herbs were also collected to supplement the many herbs used in product preparation. Herbs were also purchased from traditional herb gatherers (not Shakers), individuals who knew where desirable plants were to be found. Supplemental gathering really helped the Shaker business when demand was at its highest.

Orders for Shaker herbs, seeds, and products were both staggeringly large and diverse. Here is a journal listing for an order made in 1848 by William Charles Brackett at the Watervliet, New York, location: *motherwort, peppermint, spearmint, thoroughwort, catnip, pennyroyal, thyme, butternut, henbane, saffron, boneset, white root, dandelion, bloodroot, spikenard root, belladonna, elder flower, lobelia, wintergreen, Solomon seal, skullcap, comfrey root, blackberry bark and root, sage, wormwood, southernwood, blue cardinal flower, bittersweet, marshmallow, tansy, thyme, hyssop, lemon balm, slippery elm, horehound, foxglove, summer savory, sweet bugle, sweet marjoram , lettuce, sweet fern, rue, ground ivy, chamomile flower, double tansy, dear elder root, loverwort, skunk cabbage roots, angelica seed, burdock roots, pleurisy root, mugwort, coltsfoot, fern root, buckthorn berries, bayberry bark, smallage, cranesbill, stramonium, frostwort, sweet flag roots, moldavian balm, goldthread, poppy flowers, poppy seed, poppy capsules, mullein, cleavers, cohosh root, yarrow, thorn apple, mayweed, coriander seed, elecampane, hemlock and oak barks, mandrake root, cranberry bark, caraway seed, indigo root, Balm of Gilead buds, hickory ash bark, wild turnip, shakehead, gold seal root, bethroot, crawly roots, cicuta, calamus root, sweet basil , rose willow bark, rose leaves, celadine, marigold flowers, garden and wild lettuce, datura, garget, ladies slipper, marsh rosemary roots, princes pine, Oak of Jerusalem, avens roots, larkspur seed, vervain, yellow dock, life everlasting, white like root, fever-few, queen of the meadow, horseradish, prickly ash, savin, Latuca virosa (poison lettuce), scabs, maidenhair fern, scurvy grass, bladderroot, John's-wort,* and *elderberry wine.*

Roots and aerial parts of herbs collected in the wild included mandrake root, sweet fern, wormwood, sweet flag, wild lettuce, boneset (also spelled bone set), comfrey root, cattail, flag, wintergreen, bugle, and skullcap. Blackberries and raspberries were also wild collected and cultivated at the communities.

The Shaker ethic included working out new and improved cultivation

Red raspberry bushes in the Food Garden at Jardin Botanique, Montreal.
Peter Coleman

practices. While wild-harvesting blackberries near the Shirley, Massachusetts, community, "Brother Leander noticed a particular vine where the berries hung ripe, having developed a full two weeks ahead of the surrounding vines. In addition, this vine was virtually free from thorns." So he marked the vine and came back after the leaves fell and transplanted the cane in the vicinity to his community for cultivation. Finding the early ripened berries was a cultivation coup. Constant experimentation improved the quantity and quality of their *Rubus* crops and other harvests, year after year.

Harvesting the various parts of *Rubus* plants was done at different times of the year. For cultivation purposes, the root was gathered in the fall after the leaves had fallen. When the root needed to be dug up and dried for preparations, it was collected in the spring before flowers appeared, or in late fall.

Rubus leaves were harvested at any time as long as they were green and healthy-looking. Shakers spread leaves on drying screens or hung bunches to dry on the canes (being careful of thorns). Young leaves and new shoots were collected in the spring while still tender, before plants started to flower. These young harvested leaves and shoots were sometimes fermented, for up to 6 weeks, then dried to make tea.

Blackberries generally ripen before raspberries and can be found from May to September, but the height of the season is in June and July. Raspberries (including black raspberries) have either an early summer crop, peaking in July, or late summer-into-autumn crop producing berries in late July or August and in the northeastern areas of the United States (where a lot of Shaker communities settled) could produce fruits up until the first frost.

Harvesting and preserving herbs entailed a lot of work. The methods Shakers used were what a typical housewife might have done before and during the Civil War era. Shaker sisters worked at large tables to perform processes involved in the harvesting and preparation of herbs. Labors included cutting down ariel plant parts, digging up roots and cleaning them, picking over flowers and plants, hanging or spreading herbs out on screens to dry, cleaning bottles, cutting and printing labels, packaging herbs and seeds, putting up syrups, ointments and extracts and more. So while this may have made more work for the Shaker sisters, it lessened the burden on the housewife to purchase their products rather than maintain a simples garden.

Distribution and Products

The Shakers had so many products to offer that they created catalogues to simplify ordering for their customers. A catalogue created around the time of the Civil War divulges the comprehensive range of items: 354 medicinal plants, barks, roots, seeds and flowers; 156 fluid extracts; 59 solid extracts; 48 ordinary extracts; 84 powdered articles, contrasted preparations, including 22 alkaloids and resinoids; 10 ointments; 7 double distilled and fragrant waters; 9 essential oils; and finally, 4 pulverized sweet herbs—sage, thyme, summer savory, and sweet marjoram.

Demand from the New World grew and became one of the most lucrative of Shaker enterprises. They were not above promoting their own goods to customers within the United States while still encouraging the European market. This little couplet was printed in a Shaker catalogue:

> *Why send to Europe's distant shore*
> *For plants which grow at our own doors?*

The Shakers sold thousands of pounds of herbs and roots a year. They put up seeds in cloth bags, retailed smaller portions in papers or envelopes (such as we have today), and started issuing specialty gardener's manuals for kitchen gardens, injurious insects, cooking recipes, preserving, and uses of vegetables.

Blackberry and Raspberry as Medicines and Food

Varieties of blackberry, raspberry and black raspberry were used in medicinal compounds and culinary recipes. The Shaker fondness for experimentation led to a slew of products like berry-based syrups, berry brandies, jams made with wild gathered fruits and berries, or fruit wines and liqueurs made with cherries, grapes, plums, elderberries, blackberries, and raspberries "for medicinal purposes or otherwise." Shoots and roots were collected to create a blue-grey dye.

Although *Rubus* fruits were used interchangeably, blackberries were more often purposed for medicinal use, while raspberries and black raspberries were more frequently pressed into culinary service. Perhaps blackberries were thought to have more medicinal value, or it was a matter of availability at production time, or a preference for flavor profile for one application over another, or even the amount of yield of one berry over another.

Blackberry root (*R. fruticosus*) was used alone or in conjunction with other herbs as a component in decoctions, wines, syrups, or teas recommended for many serious intestinal issues including colitis, dysentery, diarrhea, and cholera infantum (intestinal distress in infants and young children). Blackberry preparations could also be found in the form of fleet injections to treat gonorrhea and prolapsed uterus and anus. The root is the most astringent part of the plant making it very good for these issues. A tea made from the roots was helpful for labor pains; it was also used as a rinse for mild mouth and throat irritations.

Roots and leaves were dug, dried, and stored until needed. To treat diarrhea, prepare a medicine from the root using one teaspoon of dried, crushed root stirred into one cup of boiling water. Drink one or two cups of the cooled infusion daily until diarrhea is cleared up. Eating lots of fresh blackberries or raspberries has the same effect.

Blackberry syrups were endorsed as medicinal treatments for whooping cough, bronchitis, asthma, and other respiratory ailments. The juice was recommended for colitis, diarrhea, fluid retention, diabetes, and gout. A soothing throat syrup can be made from blackberries or raspberries: Put two cups of berries with enough water to cover, then boil till berries are soft. Add four tablespoons of sugar till the sugar is dissolved. Strain, cool, and store in a jar in the refrigerator to use. For a sore throat, take a spoonful four times a day.

Chewing the leaves helped to relieve toothaches and sometimes "offensive saliva." Gargling with berry juice also made an excellent mouthwash. Tisanes, teas, and poultices made from the strongly astringent leaves helped with internal and external pain, swelling, and inflammation for wounds, bruises, diarrhea, and hemorrhoids. The tannins in the herb tighten tissues and control bleeding. To treat external wounds, infusions and lotions with blackberry elements were used as rinses or poultices to help healing.

Raspberry (*R. idaeus*) is often known as the American red raspberry, or just plain red raspberry The black raspberry (*R. occidentalis*) is used in the same way as blackberry for medicinal treatments of the bowels, lungs, mouth, and exterior wounds. Their large amounts of fiber work as well or better than prune juice. The berries are also used to control bedwetting or incontinence and drunk as a tonic for good health and longevity.

Raspberry seed oil's anti-inflammatory properties make it useful in products like face cream, balm, sunscreen, oil, and serum to hydrate and rejuvenate skin and reduce the signs of aging like spots and wrinkles. Eating colorful and varied *Rubus* fruits has similar benefits for the skin. Properly stored, the shelf life for *Rubus* seed oil can be up to two years.

With innovative methods of cultivating, harvesting, and marketing *Rubus* varieties, the Shakers recognized the many valuable qualities of this tasty, healthful, and ornamental Herb of the Year!

References

"6 Reasons to Use Raspberry Seed Oil in your Natural Skincare Product." *School of Natural Skin Care.* Accessed July 10, 2019. www.schoolofnaturalskincare.com/6-reasons-to-use-raspberry-seed-oil-in-your-natural-skincare-products/.

"Blackberry Leaf Tea." *Susan's Sumptuous Suppers.* Accessed 7/25/19. susansumptuoussuppers.wordpress.com/2016/02/29/blackberry-leaf-tea/.

"Blackberry Remedies." Accessed 7/25/19. http://home-plant-remedies.weebly.com/blackberry-remedies.html.

"Rubus fruticosus (blackberry) use as an herbal medicine." *Pharmacognosy Review.* Accessed 7/10/19. https://www.ncbi.nlm.nih.gov/pmc/articles/PMC4127818/.

Andrews, Edward and Faith Andrews. *Fruits of the Shaker Tree of Life: Memoirs of Fifty Years of Collecting and Research.* The Berkshire Traveler Press, 1975.

Black, Cynthia. *Natural & Herbal Family Recipes.* Storey, 1997.

Collester, J. S. *Old-Fashioned Bread Puddings & Other Old-Fashioned Desserts.* Bear Wallow Books, 2008.

-----. *Old Shaker Recipes with Historic Notes.* Bear Wallow Books, 2004.

Cooke Brown, Alice. *Early American Herb Recipes.* Bonanza Books, 1966.

Miller, Amy Bess. *Shaker Herbs: A History and A Compendium.* Clarkson N. Potter, Inc., 1976.

Raspberry leaves in spring. *Gert Coleman*

Skye Suter broadcasts her fondness for art and plants through writing, lecturing, graphic design, and illustration. As a writer and illustrator, Skye contributes to the International Herb Association's annual Herb of the Year ™ publication, and other freelance projects. She lectures on herbs and related subjects to interested groups, and teaches nature classes at a local nature center.

Current ventures include writing, lecturing, and producing newsletters, including a monthly newsletter for the Staten Island Herb Society and a quarterly newsletter for the International Herb Association. Visit Skye's website anherballeaf.com to sign up for and download copies of *An Herbal Leaf Journal* and *An Herbal Leaf Monthly Message*, publications "about plants, nature, art, crafting, cooking, and especially herbs." An archive of *An Herbal Leaf* subjects is also available on the website. Skye can be reached at anherballeaf@gmail.com.

Fruiting *Rubus fruticosus* 'Chester' thornless. *Pat Kenny*

My Ruckus with *Rubus*: Rooting Out Invasive Plants

Tina Marie Wilcox

Gardening in the Arkansas Ozarks is wild and fraught with challenges. The soil consists of weathered rock. That rock is sandstone on the ridges that I cultivate. The sandstone ranges from solid slab to boulders to forms that can be used for stepping stones or building houses.

The natural flora consists of hardwood forests, prairie forbs, grasses, brambles, and invasive species of all kinds. During the growing season the weather is hot and humid. Rain events are random. Average annual precipitation is 49.6 inches.

I have lost a secret garden on the northeast side of my woodland cottage. It is situated on great slabs of sandstone. It is shaded by a male persimmon, three ancient Eastern junipers, a slippery elm, a mature white oak, and numerous hickory trees. The tree roots, along with those of other less desirable plants, fill pockets of powdery soil and humus and are wedged in between the cracks in the rocks.

The main feature of my secret garden is sitting prominently on a natural rock slab patio. This is a square slab of sandstone, with a bucket-sized hole carved out of the center, sitting atop four stone table supports that were cemented there by a stone mason long ago. The hole rock is thought to have been the covering for a hand-dug well.

The gardener who preceeded me on this land planted periwinkle, both the *Vinca major*, 'Variegata' and *V. minor*, as groundcover under the trees. Additionally, English ivy (*Hedera helix*) covers areas of the ground as well as tree trunks, and is reaching up to take up residence on the siding on the cottage. I introduced cinnamon vine, *Dioscorea polystachya*, a non-native vine with edible aerial "potatoes". This adversary spreads by means of underground tubers and by shedding potato-like bulbils which take root upon contact with soil. It winds around the stems of the other plants and the rails of my deck. This long vine has to be cut away and unwound from the supports it uses to travel and seek light.

These invasive species are drought- and deer-resistant and form thick mats that exclude the growth of most annuals and any other plants that are not exceedingly determined to compete. Having populated all possible soil deposits in the garden area, they are creeping into the Ozark forest on the north side of my home. It is my sworn responsibility to destroy these invaders before I depart this life.

Various tree seedlings and samplings, Virginia creeper (*Parthenocissus quinquefolia),* and poison ivy (*Toxicodendron radicans),* all native species, present challenges to extraction. The baby trees have to be completely uprooted or they will sprout back and be even more difficult to grub out in future years. Virgina creeper vines are easily pulled from the ground and off trees. Rooting them out, however, is similar to getting the small trees; you have to be sure to dig down and extract all of it. Gauntlet gloves, long sleeves and pants, and a pair of pliers are needed to safely extract the poison ivy; still, there is no guarantee that the gardener will complete the day without contracting a case of contact dermatitis caused by urushiol from poison ivy and other toxic oils present in many of the other offending plants.

Finally, making the reclamation project completely crazy, head high above the fray, there stand multiple arched, prickly canes of blackberries, protruding throughout the mass of meaness. I have lived with this stand since 1991. Walking through the brambles is impossible. If the berries were large and sweet, I would transplant them to a place where they could be cultivated. Instead they are seedy and sour and rarely develop a full-sized berry because they are the favorite food of stinkbugs and beetles. They serve only as the botanical guardians of the invaders of the secret garden.

I suspect each of the blackberry canes is part of one large organism, connected together by long strands of strong roots. As I approach each cane in the excavation process, working in the soil, I examine the roots of the many plants that are being extracted. This process has taught me the characteristics and appearance of each type of root. Blackberry roots are not much larger than thin sphagetti noodles, with finer side roots diverging from the main runner every several inches. The roots run about three-inches below and horizontal to the surface of the soil. The color is light brown and they are tough and fibrous.

It is possible to work with a *hori hori* under the root, flicking away small rocks and soil to follow its length as far as possible. The extraction may end at a boulder or a large tree root, making it necessary to sever the long strand, knowing that what is left will live on to produce another cane.

Given my desire to restore the magic of the secret garden and save the forest from the invasive species, I have to carefully consider my options. There are herbicides that can help. Herbicides are counterintuitive in many ways. On the other hand, given the urgency of saving the native forest from plants introduced by my predecessor and myself from possible generations of invasion, I have to make reasonable and measured use of the tools available.

Glycosphate (widely known as RoundUp®) is a systemic herbicide that kills down to the roots indiscriminately. It is most effective on perennial plants when sprayed on foliage near the end of the growing season, when the sap is sinking back to the roots. The vision of the secret garden covered in dead plants, as if an atomic weapon had been dropped, is not acceptable. Completely rooting out all of the enemies is not possible because so much of the root system is safely wedged under and between rocks.

The compromise and plan of action I have chosen is threefold. First I will root out as many of these weeds as I can by hand. These will have to be removed from the garden dead or alive so I might as well get it done now. Tree saplings that are too large to dig out will be cut and the stump will be treated with a few drops of concentrated glycosphate. I will follow the eradication efforts with a mulch of rotted leaves to protect soil life. As new weed sprouts appear, I will apply diluted glycosphate, according to label instructions, as frugally as possible. I expect this process will take a number of summers to complete. Let this ruckus with *Rubus* and its league of invaders begin.

To prepare, the first thing I do is to take care of the gardener. Before getting dressed, I drink a glass of water and then refill the container and cover it with a lid. This will keep the water handy for constant hydration while protecting the contents and my mouth from yellow jackets, dirt, and grit. Iced coffee, water kefir, and fruited vinegar with honey (commonly called *shrub*) are other liquid refreshment that are stimulants I use for hard labor.

I slather my body with coconut oil to which a few drops of vetiver, scented geranium, and cedar essential oils are added to protect myself from chigger, tick, and mosquito bites. Then I suit up in long sleeves, overalls, socks, and work boots. I spray DEET on this clothing along with my sweat cloth, gloves, and sun hat.

Next, the tools of battle are assembled. These include a *hori hori* (Japanese weeding knife), a spading fork, pruners, and pliers. A broadfork, made of alloy steel, with two 4-foot-long handles and 12-inch tines, will help me lever heavy rocks out of the way for eradicating roots and dig deeply with the force of steel and only my body weight.

The wheelbarrow is parked nearby. A bucket for most of the weeds is placed to my left. These will be wheeled out to the pasture and allowed to dry, die, and be recycled back to the land. A repurposed animal feed bag is at the ready for receiving gently cut and unwound cinnamon vines with their aerial bulblets, which will be transported to the landfill as the tubers and bulblets will not die reliably in the field.

The blackberry canes will be handled separately with gloved hands. The best place to grasp extracted blackberry canes is at the part of the stem that grows just below the soil surface—there are no prickles there. By aligning the canes in a neat stack, it is possible to transport a number of them without injury. The canes will be laid over areas in my Mediterranean Garden that my cats habitually use as a litter box. The prickles will serve as a barrier for a number of months because they remain long after the cane has dried out. Hopefully this will encourage the cats to take their business elsewhere. After the cats are trained, the dead brambles will be dragged out to the field and stacked to provide cover for wildlife until they decompose.

Finally, I put on favorite music or podcasts and sit down at the outer edge of the territory. Now it's just a matter of discipline. Root out each problem plant as completely as possible, advance, and stay happy doing it. My dog, Brynn, comes over from time to time to smell and listen to the jungle around me to make sure it is free from copperheads or other snakes.

At the end of the first day of work, the partially recaptured garden reveals a stone pathway and new, shady ground. My chickens peck around in the freshly bared soil, gobbling down earthworms and grubs. Then they scratch out saucers for their underbellies, nestle in, and fluff their wings over the mounds of moist, cool earth.

On the other side of the house in the Mediterranean Garden, my fat cat waddles over to a mound he habitually scratches up to cover his excrement. He steps back quickly from the prick his paw receives. All is well in my world and it is just a matter of time and concentrated effort until my ruckus with *Rubus* is complete and the magic is returned to the secret garden.

Tina Marie Wilcox has been the head gardener and herbalist at the Ozark Folk Center State Park's Heritage Herb Garden in Mountain View, Arkansas, since 1984. She coordinates annual herb events and facilitates the production of herb seeds and plants for the park. She co-authored the reference book, *the creative herbal home* with Susan Belsinger. She is known, nationwide, as an entertaining and enlightening herbal educator.

Professional memberships include the Herb Society of America and the International Herb Association. In 2017 she was honored with the HSA Nancy Putnam Howard Award for Excellence in Horticulture. Tina began her second term as president of IHA in 2019. Tina's philosophy is based upon experiencing the joy of the process, perpetrating no harm and understanding life through play with plants and people. braidnboots@gmail.com

Wineberry canes showing bristles. *Pat Kenny*

Eating Rubus

Baskets of freshly-picked berries. *Karen O'Brien*

Berry Month

Wilma Jozwiak

August is my month of berries this year,
The tag end now of swollen rich blueberries,
Voluptuous, popping open, crushed by hasty teeth,
Leaking out the one true taste of blue.

And dewberries, creeping vines with hair-like thorns
That show themselves as little twinges from hidden hypodermics.
Berries fat with taste and damning stains,
A taste like blackberries died and gone to heaven.

And Queen of August, blackberries sway on strong tall canes,
A baffle trap of knife-like thorns,
Hidden gems within a green-leafed cave,
I pick, and eat, and pick, and smile a stain-toothed smile.

Wilma Jozwiak is an Upstate New Yorker transplanted from East Tennessee, where she learned to love blackberries. She bears her bramble scars with pride.

Just-picked blackberries and sliced peaches are in the making for a summer fruit crumble. *Susan Belsinger*

Just Desserts
Susan Belsinger

Peach and Blackberry Crumble

There is nothing to compare with fresh, ripe peaches at the height of the summer. And they just happen to be in season when blackberries are peaking. I like combining the sweetness of peaches or nectarines with the tartness of the blackberries for a tasty fruit dessert. Adding a lemon herb is a lovely accent to the fruit, though optional if you don't have fresh herbs. I used walnuts here; however, pecans or almonds are also good. Serve with vanilla ice cream or lightly whipped cream for a delightful dessert, or with yogurt for breakfast.

Serves 8

3 ripe peaches and/or nectarines, peeled and sliced, about 1 1/4 pounds
1 quart ripe blackberries
1/4 cup pure maple syrup
1/8 cup chopped lemon verbena, lemon balm or lemon basil leaves, optional
3/4 cup unbleached or whole-wheat pastry flour
1/4 cup cornmeal
1/2 cup oats
Few pinches salt
Generous 1/4 teaspoon cinnamon
Few grindings of nutmeg
8 tablespoons unsalted butter, cut into pieces
1/4 cup organic brown sugar or maple syrup

Preheat oven to 400° F and butter a 2 1/2-quart baking dish.

Combine the peaches or nectarines with the blackberries and transfer them to the baking dish; drizzle 1/4 cup maple syrup over them. If the fruit is tart, add a little more syrup.

Combine the flour, cornmeal, oats, salt, cinnamon, and nutmeg in a bowl and stir to blend. Cut just 6 tablespoons of the butter pieces into the crisp ingredients with a pastry blender until just blended. Spread the mixture over the fruit and then sprinkle the top with chopped walnuts. Scatter the brown sugar overall or drizzle with syrup and dot with the remaining 2 tablespoons of butter.

Bake in preheated oven for about 25 to 30 minutes, until the crisp is golden brown and the fruit is bubbling. Serve warm or at room temperature.

Chocolate Shortcakes with Cocoa Whipped Cream and Raspberries

Although these are a bit unusual, they work out to be a pretty tasty combination. These biscuits are not really sweet—so don't expect a brownie. The cocoa whipped cream is wickedly decadent so just plain fruit without sweetener or syrup works best. Fresh raspberries are a naturally great partner with the chocolate.

Makes about 1 dozen 2 1/2-inch rounds

Shortcakes

2 cups unbleached white flour
6 tablespoons cocoa
3/4 teaspoon salt
3 teaspoons baking powder
1/2 teaspoon baking soda
4 tablespoons organic sugar
8 tablespoons unsalted butter
1 cup + 1 tablespoon milk
1/2 teaspoon pure vanilla extract
3/4 cup bittersweet chocolate chips

Preheat oven to 400° F. Combine the flour, cocoa, salt, baking powder, baking soda, and sugar in a bowl or processor. Cut the butter into the mixture until it is a coarse meal. Mix the milk and vanilla together. Add the milk to the dry ingredients and mix until just coming together. Sprinkle in the chocolate chips and mix until blended. Do not overmix.

Turn the dough onto a floured surface and knead 8 or 10 times, adding a little flour if need be. Roll the dough to about 3/4-inch thick. Using a 2 1/2-inch cutter, cut out rounds, using all of the dough. Place the rounds of dough on the baking sheet.

Bake the biscuits in the center of the oven for about 20 to 22 minutes; they need to cook a little longer since they are dense and have chocolate chips in them. Cool the biscuits for at least 5 minutes before splitting them open; they are best served warm, but room temperature is fine.

Cocoa Whipped Cream

1 pint heavy whipping cream
4 tablespoons unsweetened cocoa
4 to 5 tablespoons organic sugar or pure maple syrup
1 teaspoon pure vanilla extract
2 pints ripe red raspberries

In a deep bowl, combine the whipping cream and cocoa; whisk to blend in cocoa. Cover and refrigerate for one hour or overnight.

Whisk the cream until it just starts to thicken and add the sugar or whisk until soft peaks just start to form and add maple syrup. Taste for sweetener and add the additional tablespoon if need be. Whisk until soft peaks though not stiff and whisk in the vanilla extract.

Serve a dollop on each chocolate biscuit and garnish with red ripe raspberries. The cream can be made in advance and kept in the fridge—if it gets a little thin, just whisk it up again.

Summer Berry Trifle with Lemon Herb Syrup

Traditionally most trifles are made with sponge cake or lady fingers, custard, and jam. This trifle has been brought up to date—it is lighter and fresher, and quite delicious. I've used an angel food cake, fresh fruit of the season, and captured the flavor of the herbs of summer in a simple syrup.

I like to use my foraged wineberries the best in this recipe and if there aren't enough then I often combine them with sliced, dead-ripe peaches—substitute the freshest fruit available—raspberries, blackberries, blueberries, nectarines and plums all work well in this recipe. If you don't have time to bake the cake, buy one. Any of the lemon herbs—lemon balm, lemon verbena, lemongrass, or lemon basil—are wonderful or use a combination of them.

Makes 1 large trifle; about 24 servings (recipe can be easily halved)

10-inch angel food cake
1 recipe lemon herb syrup (recipe follows)
2 pints wineberries or raspberries
2 pints blackberries or blueberries
6 to 8 ripe peaches, nectarines or plums
2 tablespoons grenadine syrup
1 quart whipping cream
1/2 cup organic sugar
1 1/2 teaspoons pure vanilla extract
Lemon herbs for garnish
1 pint extra berries for garnish as well as lemon herb leaves

You will need a large, preferably clear glass, bowl. Slice the angel food cake into 3/4-inch slices; cut the slices into about 3/4-inch squares. Once the syrup has cooled, squeeze the essence from the herbs and remove them.

Rinse the wineberries, raspberries, blackberries, or blueberries only if need be and transfer them to a separate bowl. Toss the berries with the grenadine; if you don't have it then use the herb syrup (see below).

Peel and pit the stonefruits and slice them thinly. Put them in a bowl and pour a little of the syrup over them so that they do not turn dark.

Whip the cream, adding the sugar a few tablespoons at a time. Add the vanilla towards the end of the whipping; the cream should have soft peaks.

Place a layer of peaches and berries (using 1/4 of them) in the bottom of the bowl with some of the syrup. Cover them with about a quarter of the cake squares. Spoon about one-fourth of the whipping cream over the cake. Place another layer of peaches and berries over the cream, add another quarter of the cake, and then another fourth of the cream. Repeat with the peaches and berries, another quarter of the cake, and fourth of the cream. The final layer is peaches and berries, the remainder of the cake, drizzle about 1/4 to 1/2 cup syrup over all, and spoon on the remaining cream.

Keep the trifle in the refrigerator until ready to serve. Remove about 10 minutes before serving.

Decoratively garnish the top with the extra whole berries and lemon herb leaves. Serve the trifle into pretty glass bowls or glass stemware.

Lemon Herb Syrup

Herb syrups are wonderful flavor essences that can be added in place of the liquid in cakes, pie filling, and sorbet. They are good on all kinds of fruits and used in beverages. Make these when you have fresh herbs in abundance—their flavor and aroma will bring a brightness to fruits and desserts.

Makes about 2 cups

1 1/2 cups water
1 1/2 cups sugar
About 10 to 12 sprigs lemon verbena, lemon basil or lemon balm leaves or a combination thereof

To make an herb syrup, combine the water and sugar in a small saucepan and place over moderate heat and bring to a boil. Stir to dissolve sugar, add the lemon herbs and remove from heat. Cover, and let stand for at least 30 minutes.

Remove the leaves and squeeze them into the syrup to extract their flavor. This syrup can be made ahead and kept in the refrigerator for up to 2 weeks.

See bio on page 27.

Blackberries ripening. *Pat Kenny*

Raspberry Recipes for Any Time of Day

Gert Coleman

Raspberry Muffins with Pecan Streusel Topping

This recipe is delicious plain, without the topping, excellent for breakfast, lunch, dessert, or for afternoon tea with friends. The streusel topping, with or without your favorite nut, brings these muffins to a whole new level of pleasure and taste. You can make the topping the night before to speed things along in the morning. I use low-fat milk because that's what we usually have on hand. I find a quick sifting makes the muffins even lighter. Blackberries work well in this recipe, but I suggest you use a seedless variety. To be fancy, stick a raspberry on top or in the center. If making a coffeecake, bake for 1 hour and 15 minutes. Adapted from Deborah Madison's cookbook Vegetarian Cooking for Everyone *(Broadway Books 1997).*

Makes 12 to 15 muffins

Pecan Streusel Topping

3/4 cup brown sugar
4 teaspoons flour
1/2 teaspoon cardamom, optional
1/2 teaspoon cinnamon
5 tablespoons butter
1 cup chopped pecans or walnuts

Muffins

2 1/2 cups all-purpose flour
2 teaspoons baking powder
1 teaspoon baking soda
1/2 teaspoon salt
1/2 to 3/4 cup packed light brown sugar

2 eggs, lightly beaten
1 1/3 cups milk
1/3 cup olive oil or butter
1 1/2 teaspoons vanilla extract
1 cup fresh raspberries, or frozen, partially thawed

Preheat oven to 375° F. Oil or butter the muffin tins.

For the topping, mix together the brown sugar, flour, spices, butter, and nuts using two knives to cut in the butter or in a food processor until crumbly. Set aside. Refrigerate if not using right away.

For the muffins, mix flour, baking powder, baking soda, salt, and brown sugar in one bowl. Mix eggs, milk, oil or butter, and vanilla extract in a smaller bowl. Using a rubber spatula, stir batter up from bottom of the bowl to make sure there are no pockets of flour. Do not beat the batter; it may look uneven.

Drop raspberries into batter and mix to coat lightly. Scoop batter into tins, going nearly to the top for a nicely rounded muffin. Sprinkle streusel topping over the batter, pressing lightly into it, just before they go in the oven.

Bake in the upper third of the oven until browned and well risen, about 25 minutes. Turn out the muffins and serve with butter or jam.

Ceil's Raspberry Bread Pudding

I've adapted my sister's recipe to use red raspberries instead of blueberries. Bread that is a few days old will absorb the egg-milk mixture better than fresh. Regular sugar is fine, but if you have some vanilla sugar, the dish is even better. I add a dash of cardamom because I have fallen in love with this aromatic spice. For a richer custard, use 2 cups half-and-half and 2 cups milk.

16-ounce loaf challah, brioche, or other egg bread, cubed
6 eggs
1 cup plus 1 tablespoon sugar
4 cups milk (or 2 cups half-and-half and 2 cups milk)
1/4 cup butter, melted
1/2 teaspoon ground cinnamon
1/4 teaspoon ground nutmeg
Dash cardamom, optional
1 cup fresh raspberries

Butter a large baking dish and set aside. Cube the bread into 1 1/2-half inch pieces. Place half the bread into the prepared dish and sprinkle with half the raspberries. Top with remaining bread and raspberries.

In a large bowl, whisk the eggs. Gradually add in 1 cup of the sugar until thoroughly combined and no sugar is sitting on the bottom of the bowl. Whisk in the milk, melted butter, cinnamon, nutmeg, and cardamom (if using).

Pour mixture over the bread and raspberries, pressing bread down gently to absorb the liquid. Cover dish with plastic wrap and refrigerate for an hour or longer. (For a bright, berry breakfast dish, you can leave overnight in the refrigerator.)

Heat oven to 350° F. Take pudding dish from the refrigerator and remove plastic wrap. Sprinkle evenly with the remaining sugar.

Bake for 1 hour, until top is browned nicely and the pudding is puffed. Let cool for 10 to 15 minutes then serve with whipped cream or vanilla ice cream.

German Apple-Berry Pancake

I've made this dramatic one-dish pancake with a variety of fruits since the 1970s when I first bought Anna Thomas' the vegetarian epicure *(Vintage Books 1972). The book is stained and held together with rubber bands, but the recipe has become a family favorite. Typically served for breakfast, we have also eaten it for dinner and served it as dessert. If you don't have fresh berries, you can use frozen, but thaw them slightly first.*

Makes 4 servings

Pancake

3 large eggs
1 cup milk
1 cup white flour
1/2 teaspoon salt, optional
1 1/2 tablespoons butter

Filling

6 tart fresh apples, peeled and sliced
1/4 cup melted butter
1/4 cup sugar
Dash cinnamon, optional
1 cup fresh raspberries

Preheat oven to 450° F. Beat together the eggs, milk, flour, and salt until very smooth. In a heavy 12-inch skillet, melt 1 1/2 teaspoons butter. As soon as it is quite hot, pour in the batter and put the skillet in the oven.

After 15 minutes, lower the oven temperature to 350° F and continue baking for another 20 minutes. The pancake should be light brown and crisp. During the first 20 minutes, the pancake may puff up in large bubbles. Pierce it thoroughly with a skewer or knife.

While the pancake is baking, prepare the fruit filling. Peel and thinly slice the apples and sauté them lightly in 1/4 cup butter, about 8 to 10 minutes. Stir in 1/4 cup sugar. Season with cinnamon, if desired. Add the raspberries during the last few minutes of cooking to keep them whole but warmed through.

When the pancake is ready, remove from the oven and pour the filling over the pancake. Slice and serve with whipped cream or maple syrup.

Summer Easy Berry-Nut Chocolate Dessert

Raspberries and dark chocolate have a special affinity for each other. If you add walnuts, you can savor this for a light summer lunch or save it for dessert. My sister likes to add coconut flakes.

2 pints fresh raspberries
1 bar 70% organic dark chocolate, chopped into small bits
1 cup chopped walnuts, optional
2 sprigs fresh mint, chopped

In a pretty glass bowl, mix together the berries, chocolate, and mint. Sprinkle walnuts on top, if using.

See bio on page 67.

Where the berries meet the sea. *Bonny Lundy*

Brambleberry Bumble

Pat Crocker

Bumble. It's a word I've coined to describe berries baked with honey and a crumbly topping. In Canada, we make berry or apple cobbler, crumble, crisp, grunt, buckle, and pandowdy. Why not add another descriptive? In Eastern Canada, we gather foxberries, black or choke cherries, bunchberries, and huckleberries. Saskatoon and silver buffalo berries reign in the west. And right here in Ontario and Quebec, we gather wild blueberries (smaller and tarter than domestic varieties), as well as elderberries, cranberries, blackberries, and wild or escaped raspberries. Excerpted from Spring 2014 IHA newsletter.

Makes 4 servings

Bumble Filling

5 cups fresh or frozen raspberries or blackberries
1 teaspoons freshly squeezed lemon juice
1/3 cup honey or coconut nectar
2 tablespoons all-purpose flour

Topping

1/2 cup butter or soft coconut oil
2 tablespoons all-purpose flour
1/2 cup coconut sugar or brown sugar
1 1/4 cups large flake rolled oats
1/2 teaspoon cinnamon

Preheat oven to 375° F. Grease an 8-inch baking dish and toss berries, lemon juice, honey and flour together. Spread mixture evenly over the bottom of the dish.

In a bowl, using a wooden spoon, cream butter, flour and sugar together. Stir in rolled oats, cinnamon, and salt and mix until crumbly. Spread evenly over berries in the dish.

Bake in preheated oven for 25 to 30 minutes or until top is golden and berries are bubbling.

Gail Wood Miller

Pat Crocker and her recipes look best in black. She cherishes the many *Rubus* varieties growing wild in her native Grey County, Ontario, Canada. Culinary herbalist, photographer, writer, lecturer and author of several award-winning books, Pat's latest book, *The Herbalist's Kitchen* is now available in bookstores everywhere and on her website: www.patcrocker.com.

Red Raspberries, My Favorite Fruit

Donna Frawley

Raspberries truly are my favorite fruit. I love raspberries! I have picked them in the wild, grown cultivated plants in my garden, and gone to "You pick" farms to gather raspberries. I have used them to make jam, jelly, syrup, pies, tarts, sorbet, ice cream, and raspberry vinegar; as a topping on ice cream; and added dried raspberries to one of my bestselling mixes, *Raspberry and White Chocolate Sweet Mix*. While I have also grown a variety of blackberries, the production was low, and the long, thorny stems seemed to grab onto any clothing coming within a foot of it. We removed them and used the space for something more productive.

When I was a small girl visiting my grandmother, she and I would walk about half a block to visit an older lady my grandmother called "Grandma Johnson." She grew flavorful raspberries and them in sold pint boxes. My grandmother was a regular customer. When we brought the berries back to my Grandma's house, she served them with cream and a sprinkling of sugar. That was the best treat ever!

After my husband and I were married, we visited his parents who lived in the same town and had a house in a wooded area. Across the street grew wild raspberries. I picked them on a regular basis and used them on cereal or made jam if I had enough for a recipe. The wild ones had bugs in them but lowering a colander full of berries into a sink of water usually made them float and I would scoop them off the top of the water and proceed with the jam-making.

Raspberries like to grow in full sun where it is not too wet and not too dry. After planting, cut the canes down to nine inches to encourage new growth. The second year you will have fruit. They are self-fertile so you only need one bush to have fruit, but you will want more than one bush if you love raspberries like I do. Pruning raspberry bushes is essential. Berries form on second year canes and when the season is over, the fruit-bearing canes die

Pail of wineberries: rubyfruit jungle. *Susan Belsinger*

and need to be pruned to the ground as soon as they are done bearing fruit. The canes that were new that year will bear the fruit the following growing season, and on it goes.

You also need to mulch raspberries to help conserve moisture and keep the weeds down. They should be planted in a row for easier maintenance, like weeding, mulching, and removing suckers. Suckers that spring up outside of the rows should be removed, for they take nutrients from the main bush and will reduce the overall production as well as make harvesting more difficult.

I also use raspberry leaves in my Relaxing Tea, one of the teas I sell. At earthfriends.com, Amy Rose details the benefits of red raspberry leaf tea. This description makes me think we all need to drink red raspberry leaf tea! "The tea leaves are naturally high in magnesium, potassium, iron and B vitamins. It's helpful for nausea and leg cramps (which may improve sleep). It also has astringent properties, which make it soothing, for your insides and your outsides. Anyone can use it for sunburn, eczema, rashes, and other skin irritations and can improve gum disease. It is also high in vitamins C, and E which are helpful for their immune properties and for energy. It is a great detoxifier, which is beneficial to men and women. We are exposed to hormones every day in the foods we consume that are laden with estrogen in the form of soy; even oil sprays have soy in the propellant. Regular use helps detoxify these hormones and may even help improve testosterone levels. The best part is, it's completely safe to use, even in large doses (see pregnancy section for a possible exception) and is even safe for children."

For culinary uses of red raspberries, the following recipes are some of my favorites.

Raspberry Vinegar

Fill a jar (whatever size you choose) half full of raspberries. Cover with the vinegar of your choice to fill the jar. Cover with the lid—if it is metal, use a barrier of plastic wrap or a small plastic bag over the jar before screwing on the metal lid so the vinegar doesn't corrode the metal. Write the date and the type of vinegar on a label, adhere it to the jar, and store it in a cool dark place for 3 to 4 weeks. When the 3 to 4 weeks are up, pour liquid through a coffee filter to filter off berries, any soil that may have been on the berries, and any pests that may have come along for the ride. When filtering is complete, pour vinegar into a plain jar or decorative bottle.

Use in any recipe that calls for Raspberry Vinegar. The following two are great!

Salad with Creamy Raspberry Vinaigrette

This vinaigrette is good on any salad, even a chef's salad, and keeps in the refrigerator for one to two weeks.

Makes 4 to 6 servings

Vinaigrette

2 tablespoons poppy seeds
3/4 cup mayonnaise
1/3 cup sugar
2 tablespoons Raspberry Vinegar
1/4 cup milk
1/4 cup olive oil

Put all vinaigrette ingredients in a jar and shake.

Salad

10 cups Romaine greens
2 cups strawberries, sliced
1 medium red onion, sliced
2 cups mandarin oranges, drained
1 cup slivered almonds, toasted

Put all salad ingredients in a large salad bowl. Pour on vinaigrette and toss.

Mixed Greens with Warm Raspberry Dressing

This can also be made using olive oil in place of the bacon fat.

Makes 4 servings

4 slices of bacon, cut up and fried until crispy, reserving 2 tablespoons bacon fat
3 tablespoons Raspberry Vinegar
2 tablespoons raspberry jam
6 cups mixed greens

In a frypan combine reserved bacon fat, jam, and vinegar. Heat until bubbling, stirring constantly. Cook down until slightly thick. Put greens in a bowl, sprinkle on bacon, pour on dressing, and toss.

No-Churn Raspberry Ice Cream

The great thing about no-churn ice cream is it easy to put together and your hands are free while it is freezing. With churn ice cream, you are slowly whipping the cream while freezing it. This cream is whipped first and then frozen. It is light and fluffy when you put it in the freezer and the air whipped into the cream keeps the ice cream easy to scoop after it is frozen.

Makes 10 to 12 servings; about 2 quarts

2 cups heavy cream
14-ounce can sweetened condensed milk
1 tablespoon vanilla extract
1 cup pureed or mashed raspberries

In a large bowl, using a hand mixer or a stand mixer, whip the cream until stiff peaks form. Be careful not to overwhip. In another large bowl, whisk the vanilla into the sweetened condensed milk; stir in pureed raspberries. Gently fold puree into the whipped cream with a rubber or silicon scraper, slowly incorporating the two mixtures together so it stays light and aerated. Pour into 9- x 5-inch loaf pan or other 2-quart container; cover. Freeze 6 hours or until firm.

Raspberry Ice

The first time I had this was over 35 years ago. My oldest sister, Penny, made this with her home-grown raspberries and I never forgot how wonderful it tasted and wanted to share it with you. I add lemon balm or lemon verbena for a bit more zest.

Makes 6 to 8 servings, or about a quart

1 teaspoon unflavored gelatin
3/4 cup sugar
1 cup water
10 ounces raspberries, frozen
2 to 3 tablespoons minced fresh lemon balm or lemon verbena
1 egg white, stiffly beaten

Mix gelatin and sugar in saucepan. Stir in water, berries, and lemon herb. Bring to a boil. Cool. Pour into an ice cube tray or an 8- by 8-inch pan. Freeze to a mush. Beat in a chilled bowl until fluffy. Fold in beaten egg white. Return to tray. Freeze until firm, 2 to 3 hours, stirring occasionally to break up the ice crystals.

Donna Frawley started her business in 1983 by selling herbs at her local farmers' market. Having majored in Home Economics and worked at a private country club, she used those skills to develop 60 culinary herb blends, 8 herb-flavored vinegars, and 8 herbal teas. She carries bulk culinary herbs and spices plus fresh herbs that are sold at LaLonde's Market and Eastman Party Store in Midland, Michigan. You can purchase her culinary mixes at www.frawleysfineherbary.com.

She has written three books, *The Herbal Breads Cookbook, Our Favorite Recipes,* and *Edible Flowers Book*, she created the DVD *Cooking with Herbs,* and writes a monthly herb column in her local newspaper. March 2010 she had her first magazine article published in *Herb Companion*. Donna hosts cooking parties, teaches cooking classes, and speaks on many culinary herb topics. She is a regular instructor at Whiting Forest in Midland, Michigan. Donna's historical fiction novel *Weymouth Place*, set in Dubuque, Iowa, from 1860 to 1875, is due out in 2021.

Donna is a member of the Valley Herb Society, the Great Lakes Herb Business Association, the Michigan Herb Associates and the IHA.

Raspberries are hollow since they leave their achene on the plant, while blackberries come off the plant and the achene remains within.
Susan Belsinger

Green berries in Art Tucker's Delaware garden. *Susan Belsinger*

Chasing the Wild Berry: Chiggers, Thorns, and Ticks, Oh, My!

Stephen Lee, the HerbMeister

City boys like me didn't get many opportunities to run amok in the wild, so my family's annual late summer trip to my father's western Kentucky hometown of Fancy Farm was always an anticipated event.

Fancy Farm is a village that sits about ten miles northwest of the Graves County seat of Mayfield which is about twenty-five miles south of Paducah, the state's sixteenth largest city, so if I say, the middle of nowhere, it isn't much of an exaggeration.

On the first Saturday of August, the village is the site of the annual St. Jerome Catholic Church Picnic, which has become quite famous over the years as both the traditional political gathering—attracting statewide and occasionally national candidates offering up rousing "stump" speeches AND the "World's Largest Picnic" as recognized by the *Guinness Book of World Records* for the consumption of about 15,000 pounds of barbequed mutton, pork, and chicken by about 15,000 people on one day each year.

The picnic has been happening since 1881. My father missed only two during his eighty-eight years on this earth and that was due to his military service during the big war. I never missed any as a child in my father's house—it was always an amazing adventure to be had.

By the time I could remember much, Grandmother Vetrice had come from the farm to Louisville to live with us and save my father from my mother's cooking—or at least that is the story we were told. In actuality, my mother was orphaned as a baby and had never received any culinary opportunities in her institutional upbringing. She would be the first to tell you that having Grandmother with us was a real blessing.

A few days before the big picnic we would all pack into the beast, our Buick Wagon Master station wagon, and head west. It was a long journey, I couldn't begin to tell you how many times one of my siblings or I asked if we were there yet—but I do remember my father saying if anybody asked that again he was going to tie them up on the roof.

We always stopped at the Kountry Kastle in Paducah for supper. It was owned by Lake Edwards who was my father's uncle and possibly best friend ever. They had joined the Army together and could tell some really hairy stories when they were celebrating over a cold beer. Lake always laid a meal of delicious smoked mutton shoulder with rye bread and shaved raw onion out before us and we devoured it like the locusts we were.

There were no hotels, motels, or Airbnbs in those days–but there was my grandmother's brother Uncle Rubel and his bride Aunt Josey's rambling old farmhouse up on the double hill, and that is always where we landed.

Having arrived very late in the evening, we were quickly ushered straight to our beds. After a great night's sleep, we woke, rested from our long travels, to the most wondrous aromas of Aunt Josey's and my grandmother's country breakfast. No time was lost getting to the kitchen and diving into mounds of hot biscuits, sausage gravy, iron skillet-fried eggs, and surely half a hog of crisply fried bacon. Yum! This glorious meal was both advance payment and ample fortification for the required work that was to follow.

In order to help feed all those barbequed-meat-eating picnic visitors, the local church women were each tasked with providing a minimum of a dozen homemade pies and at least six big cakes of some type or another to offer up on the dessert board. And, my friends, that is where berries come into this little story.

Uncle Rubel would gather us youngsters from the breakfast table and lead us down to the big, worn-red barn and there in the old harness room he would perform the pre-berry-picking ritual of tying the bottoms of our long jeans tight to our legs with thin straps of an old inner tube and douse us with a heavy sprinkling of apple cider vinegar—telling us this was the armor necessary for the bramble battles to come. He'd then hand each of us a well-used, two-quart galvanized, handled pail and point us into the woods toward the creek with the admonishment that no person was to return to the farmhouse until their pail was over-flowing with whatever berries the Good Lord had provided us that day for the church picnic pie-baking waiting to happen.

We followed the trail toward the woods, down to the creek—which wasn't much this time of year, hopped over, ran through the big meadow, and entered another world. My older brother and youngest sister (to whom he had been assigned) headed north, my two middle siblings went east, and my youngest brother and I traveled west.

Ozark hedgerow of wild blackberries. *Susan Belsinger*

It didn't take long to find the first tangled, straggly clump near the dirt-rutted road heading to the tobacco fields just past the fruit tree grove. To my memory we mostly found blackberries, but I remember a few times when we stumbled through some thickets and found thorny brambles full of those delicate red raspberries—they were harder to gather, it seemed that for every berry you picked two fell to the ground. They were Aunt Josey's favorite and she would lay great esteem upon those who returned with a clean quart or two or three of ripe, red raspberries.

We would return to the farmyard after a few hours' effort somewhat ruffled, occasionally ragged, and oft-times well-scratched. We would march triumphantly up the back steps into the screened porch and offer our overflowing pails for the inspection and praise of the elder ladies who were busy snapping the dinner green beans.

When the kudos ended, we were sent immediately back to the barn where we would strip to our skivvies to be searched for possible ticks and to locate any chigger bites or a collection of them. No matter all the precautions, there were always chigger bites and scratching. I remember well the feel of the calming calamine lotion and the not-unpleasant smell of kerosene. In retrospect—once the work and pain was over and the chigger-bite healing done—all you really remember is the sweet taste of a warm, fresh berry pie.

Uncle Rubel's farmland was blessed with an abundance of nature's bounty. It seemed something always needed to be harvested. Over the years I learned to tie and stand timothy-grass for the steers, to spear sheaves of green tobacco for hanging and drying, to climb rickety ladders for top-picking peaches and apples, and to use the new milking machines during the one time I was loaned to my Cousin Danny who operated the dairy farm next door.

In exchange for this week of farmhand effort, we were given plenty of time to explore and roam and to just rest and to eat. The women in my family were all amazing cooks–I look back fondly on so many great meals, not only during that annual week on the farm but most of my growing-up life.

When the wild raspberries and blackberries were plentiful, my grandmother, Aunt Josey, and my mother would use them for many culinary creations–not just pies. They made jellies and jams and jam cakes. They had also learned from our English forebears to make chutneys, relishes, ketchups, and vinegars. Here is one of my favorite Sunday suppers from those days on the farm using a tasty vinegar and Uncle Rubel's little secret.

Chicken in Red Berry Vinegar Sauce

Makes 8 pieces

4-pound chicken, cut into 8 pieces
Kosher salt
Freshly ground black pepper
2 tablespoons olive oil
6 tablespoons unsalted butter
2 garlic cloves, peeled and minced
4 shallots, peeled and minced
1 cup raspberry vinegar or Red Berry Vinegar*
1 teaspoon honey
1 cup white wine or Red Berry Wine**
1 tablespoon tomato paste
1 cup chicken broth

1 tablespoon fresh Italian parsley, chopped
Fresh red raspberries, for garnish

Season chicken with salt and pepper. Heat the olive oil and 2 tablespoons of the butter in a large heavy skillet over medium-high heat. Add the chicken skin side down and brown, turning once about 10 minutes per side. Remove chicken from pan and reserve.

Reduce heat to medium, add the garlic and shallots and cook, stirring often, until slightly soft, about 5 minutes. Combine the red berry vinegar with the honey and use it and the wine to deglaze the pan, scraping any browned bits from the bottom of the pan. Reduce mixture by one-third, about 3 minutes, then stir in the tomato paste.

Return chicken to the pot and pour in the chicken broth. Continue cooking over medium heat until juices from the chicken run clear, about 15 minutes. Add more chicken broth if the sauce becomes too thick.

Remove chicken to a deep serving platter. Increase heat to high and continue cooking until the sauce is thick and glossy. Remove from heat and add the remaining butter. Whisk well and adjust seasoning with salt and pepper. Pour over chicken, sprinkle with the parsley and any fresh red raspberries that may be available.

*Note: Aunt Josey would put 3 cups of apple cider vinegar into a quart jar and add 1 cup of red raspberries fresh from the brambles, just rinsed from the road dust we kicked up bringing them home, and a pinch of salt. She would put the lid on and gently shake and let the jar sit on the porch railing in the afternoon sun for about 1 hour. She said if you let it sit in the sun longer than that it would just kill the fresh berry flavor. I have learned over the years to use a white wine vinegar for a cleaner berry flavor, but Aunt Josey used cider vinegar because that is what they made and that is what they had and it was pretty darn tasty.

**Note: Uncle Rubel wasn't a true moonshiner but he did make a few barrels of wine–quite a few barrels and hard cider too. My dad said it was his little secret—but most folks knew about it and that he got the money for his new '62 John Deere peddling quarts around the county. There are no liquor stores in Graves County to this day so I don't know what they might be drinking as Uncle Rubel went to his great reward about twenty years ago. You can use a good white wine for this recipe if you don't have a nice raspberry wine on hand.

Wild Blackberry Hand Pies

Blackberry Hand Pies are not only pretty and delicious, they are simple to make and most everybody loves them. I remember them mostly as an after-school treat or what I would take to Cub Scout meetings when it was my turn.

I have always loved eating with my hands and I find the idea of hand food very intriguing and fun. It must have something to do with my English heritage. The origin of the hand pie comes from the mining Cornish who took meat and potato pasties deep into the earth for sustenance while they dug the black gold, then passed the idea to their kin as they migrated to northern Michigan and who would eventually drop them into America's melting pot cuisine.

This type of pie is resurging now into new light with the emergence of food trucks and their multitude of other hand-held foods. But if you disagree with my tactile leanings, you can easily use this recipe and make a whole pie as blackberries are great for any tart, turnover, or pie.

This pastry recipe is amazingly simple, and the dough is smooth and elastic and comes very crisp out of the oven. Remember to press the dough well together so the filling doesn't burst out while you bake them. And don't forget the three air holes to let the steam out while they are baking.

The pies are best when they are warm, but if you bake them in advance you can simply put them in a hot oven for a few minutes to warm them up. You can also freeze the pies "raw" and then bake one or two at a time.

Makes 6 pies

Filling

12 ounces wild blackberries, well rinsed and drained
3 tablespoons sugar
1 tablespoon cornstarch
1 tablespoon blackberry wine or liqueur

Crust

2 cups all-purpose flour
8 tablespoons unsalted butter, kept very cold, cut into 8 pieces
1 tablespoon sugar
1 teaspoon salt
6 tablespoons ice water
1 large egg

Put the blackberries into a heavy-bottomed saucepan and sprinkle the sugar over. Turn the heat to medium and gently shake the pan from time to time. When the sugar has melted and the berries have softened, sprinkle the cornstarch over and gently stir to incorporate. Do not overstir as you want to keep the berries as whole as possible and not cook to a jam. Add the blackberry wine, then mix and cook for 1 minute more. Remove from heat and let cool to room temperature. Filling can be made ahead and refrigerated until ready to use.

Put the flour, butter, sugar and salt into the work bowl of a food processor and pulse until the mixture comes to a "sandy" consistency. Add the ice water and pulse just until the dough begins to stick together. Put the dough out onto a clean work surface ad press it together. Do not knead the dough; simply press the crumbs together forming a flat, round disk. Wrap the dough with plastic wrap and put into the refrigerator of a minimum of 1 hour.

Preheat oven to 375°F and line baking sheet with parchment paper.

Divide the dough into 6 equal pieces. Select 1 piece and roll out to about a 4 1/2-inch round. Place 1/6 of the filling in the middle and fold the dough over. Fold the dough a little short so that you can still see a little of the bottom layer. Gently press the dough closed around the filling, using your fingertips. Now fold the overhand up and over and press down. Make a crimped edge by placing thumb and forefinger of one hand on the edge and using your index finger on the other to push a small notch into the pinched dough. Continue pinching and notching all the way around. Place the formed turnover onto the prepared baking sheet and continue making more hand pies with the remaining dough and filling.

Break the egg into a small bowl and whisk lightly. Brush the top of each pie with the egg and sprinkle with a little additional sugar. Cut 3 slits into the top of each pie and bake for about 25 minutes or until the tops are nicely browned. Remove from oven, allow to cool slightly and transfer to a wire rack to cool completely.

Wild Berry and Banana Overnight Oats

It really is true that everything old is new again. Breakfast as a child growing up in the big house on Oak Street was often frantic with so many folks heading off in every direction. My grandmother, the queen of kitchen management, took every possible shortcut to make her day more workable and may well have invented the "overnight oats category." Though, I am pretty sure she told stories of having eaten a like concoction in her youth. If you haven't tried overnight oats, you are in for a unique and pleasant experience.

Makes 1 serving

1/2 cup old-fashioned rolled oats
1/2 cup milk
1 teaspoon vanilla extract
1/2 cup wild blackberries or raspberries or both
1/2 ripe banana, sliced
Honey

Put oats into a sealable container and pour in the milk and vanilla. Add the berries and banana slices and gently mix around with a large spoon. Top with a heavy drizzle of honey and put on lid. Place in the refrigerator and let sit for 8 hours or overnight. Serve direct from the container.

Note: if peaches were in season they would often be substituted for the banana and if grandmother was in the mood she might add a tablespoon of walnuts or almonds just before eating for a little extra crunch. This recipe makes 1 serving but Grandmother made the mixture in a large batch and then divided it up into smaller containers for morning ease. It is a mixture best eaten within 24 hours—unless you really like that fermented taste.

Fresh blackberries for pastries and pies. *Susan Belsinger*

Known as the *HerbMeister*, **Stephen Lee** has enjoyed a diverse culinary career consistently interwoven with his love of herbs. He is the author of five books, including *About 8 Herbs* and *Go Withs*. He founded and operated The Cookbook Cottage, an internationally known source for rare and out-of-print cookbooks and Kentucky's first and only cooking school for fifteen years.

Twice Chairman of the Cooking Schools and Teachers Committee of the International Association of Culinary Professionals, Stephen recently retired as the director of the Daily Lunch Program for the Homeless for the Archdiocese of Louisville. He is Superintendent of the Culinary Department of the Kentucky State Fair; a licensed and active Auctioneer/Appraiser in both Indiana and Kentucky; a Board Member of the IHA Foundation; and an honest-to-goodness Kentucky Colonel. Learn more at *www.herbmeister.com*.

Fresh wineberries, high in nutrition but low in calories. *Susan Belsinger*

Two Raspberry Salsa Recipes
Jim Long

Not too many years ago, catsup was the top-selling condiment. Since that time, salsa has won the hearts of America's food lovers, as we put it on everything from chips to burgers to all kinds of main dishes. Traditionally made from tomatoes, peppers, and onions, salsa has evolved to include a wide array of vegetables, fruits, and herbs, including raspberries and other *Rubus* varieties. Use fresh or frozen red raspberries for these recipes. Both are high in nutrition, with vitamins and minerals coming from fresh ingredients, and low in calories, too. Excerpted from *Sensational Fresh Salsa from Apple to Zucchini,* copyright ©Jim Long 2016.

Raspberry Salsa

The flavor is summery and goes well with roast turkey, fish, or chips.

Yields 3 cups

3 green onions, chopped
1/2 jalapeño pepper, diced
1 small clove garlic, minced
1/2 cup fresh cilantro, chopped
Juice of two fresh limes
1 to 2 teaspoons brown sugar
2 cups fresh or frozen red raspberries

Mix all ingredients except raspberries, adding those at the very last so they stay as whole as possible. Chill for an hour before serving.

Raspberry Mango Salsa

Mangoes and raspberries combine to make a very tasty salsa or side salad for a variety of dishes.

Yields 5 cups

3 cups fresh or frozen red raspberries
2 cups fresh mango, diced
1/2 cup jicama, diced
3 green onions, diced
1 jalapeño or serrano pepper, diced
Juice of two fresh limes
2 tablespoons orange juice (or 1 tablespoon frozen concentrate)
1/4 cup fresh cilantro, chopped
1 teaspoon brown sugar
Dash of salt

Mix and chill until ready to serve.

Jim Long has been passionate about herbs since early childhood. In those years exploring native plants along the Osage River and the Taberville Prairie region of Missouri, he trained and worked as an artist and landscape designer. Jim gathered unusual plants and researched their culinary and medicinal uses. He studied cooking in Thailand and lectured at the first International Slow Food Conference in Turin, Italy, along with Michael Pollan and Alice Waters. His wealth of knowledge has earned him friendships and working relationships with some of the country's leading plant authorities. A distinguished gardener and author, Jim has published over a dozen culinary books using herbs. Visit his website at LongCreekHerbs.com to check out his books and products.

Crème de la Crop: *Rubus* Rules
Cooper T. Murray

As children, we always relished the picking of berries and popping the sweet berries into our mouths. As an adult, I grow blackberries and raspberries not far from my mint, basil, thyme, and other herbs. I have to remind myself that these little gems are indeed an herb.

Celebrating the genus *Rubus* as Herb of the Year™ 2020 could not have come at a better time. These delicious, well-known berries have always been favored. With the Paleo and Keto diets being ever so popular, raspberries and blackberries are being incorporated into a wide variety of recipes bringing many health benefits.

Eating a healthy diet and working to create delightful nutritious recipes, I have learned to bring *Rubus* berries into a wide array of dishes. Favorites are salads and vinaigrettes. But why stop there when wonderful appetizers and entrées can highlight these superfoods? I have always cherished educating others about recipes that encompass this family of herbs through my business, Organic Herbal Cooking.

The delicate, little juicy pockets of my favorite blackberries, raspberries, and marionberries are full of goodness. Please enjoy the following *Rubus* recipes, as they really are the crème de la crop. What a pleasing and beneficial herb we honor!

Grilled Flatbread Pizza with Blackberries and Arugula. *Cooper T. Murray*

Grilled Flatbread Pizza with Blackberries and Arugula

When the weather invites us to grill and spend time on the patio, this flatbread pizza with berries is an enjoyable appetizer. This recipe calls for blackberries and blueberries, but any seasonal Rubus berries will add a tasty freshness. I prefer store-bought pizza dough to save time.

Serves 6

Balsamic Reduction

1/2 cup balsamic vinegar
2 tablespoons honey

In a small saucepan, stir together the balsamic vinegar and honey. Bring to a boil, reduce heat, and simmer for 10 minutes. Set aside and let cool.

Grilled Flatbread Pizza

1/4 cup vegetable oil
1-pound ball pizza dough, room temperature
1 tablespoon flour
2 tablespoons olive oil
1 cup shredded fontina cheese
1 cup shaved Parmigiano-Reggiano cheese
1 pint blackberries
1 pint blueberries
1 cup baby arugula leaves
3 teaspoons olive oil for topping
1/4 teaspoon salt and ground pepper

Prepare the grill—clean and oil grates with vegetable oil. Heat grill to medium high heat. Roll the pizza dough into a rectangle about 1/4-inch thick. Transfer to a rimless cookie sheet or pizza paddle dusted with flour. Prick the dough with a fork, piercing all over the crust. Slide the flatbread onto the oiled grates. Close the lid and cook for about 3 minutes. Grill marks add a nice touch. If the dough puffs up, pierce with a fork to deflate. Use tongs to flip the dough and grill for 2 minutes on the second side.

Remove flatbread from the grill and brush top with olive oil. Top with fontina cheese, Parmigiano-Reggiano, blackberries, blueberries, and arugula. Drizzle with olive oil. Cut into wedges and lightly top with balsamic reduction.

Salad with Nectarines and Blackberry Vinaigrette

This year my thornless Navajo Blackberries had an incredible harvest. The bushes are 3 1/2 years old, never requiring spraying. The blackberries are large, sweet, and delicious. Another positive about the Navajo blackberry is that the berries will keep in the fridge for up to 3 weeks. Salads are always on the menu at my house, so creating a blackberry vinaigrette just made perfect sense. Add grilled chicken or shrimp to this colorful salad for a light refreshing entrée.

Serves 4

Blackberry Vinaigrette

1/2 cup blackberries
1/2 cup balsamic vinegar
1/4 cup olive oil
Zest of 1 lemon
1 tablespoon lemon juice
1 teaspoon honey
1/2 teaspoon fresh thyme, minced
1/4 teaspoon salt
1/4 teaspoon black pepper

Place the blackberries and balsamic vinegar in a small sauce pan. Simmer over medium heat for 8 minutes. While simmering, mash the blackberries. Remove from heat and strain the mixture. Place blackberry liquid in a blender. Add olive oil, lemon zest, lemon juice, honey, thyme, salt and pepper. Blend until smooth. Place in refrigerator for 10 minutes. Dressing can be made up to 1 day ahead.

Salad

8 cups baby arugula and spinach leaves
1 cup sliced nectarines
1 cup blackberries
1/4 cup roasted, sliced almonds

Divide salad greens onto 4 plates. Top with nectarines, blackberries, and sliced almonds. Drizzle with blackberry vinaigrette.

Raspberry and Basil Chicken. *Cooper T. Murray*

Raspberry and Basil Chicken

In the heat of Alabama's summer, growing raspberries may be questioned. I have had good luck planting my bushes in part shade softening the afternoon sun. One of my favorites is the Latham Red Raspberry, very hardy, and always full of beautiful berries. Fragrant leafy herbs and fresh berries complement each other wonderfully. With a garden full of sweet basil and plump raspberries ready to pick, it was time to make dinner. I decided chicken would be great as the accompaniment.

Serves 6

6 boneless chicken breasts
Olive oil or cooking spray
1/4 teaspoon salt
1/4 teaspoon black pepper
6 ounces brie
12 basil leaves, plus 6 leaves for garnish
2 pints raspberries, divided
2 tablespoons balsamic vinegar

Preheat oven to 400º F. Spray a 13- x 9-inch baking dish with cooking spray. Add chicken in a single layer, and sprinkle with salt and pepper. Remove rind from brie and cut into 6 slices. Top chicken with brie, basil, half the raspberries, and balsamic vinegar. Bake for 30 minutes, until chicken is cooked through.

Mash cooked raspberries with fork, add remaining fresh raspberries and more basil for garnish. Excellent served with quinoa or wild rice.

Roasted Raspberry Chipotle Shrimp Skewers. *Cooper T. Murray*

Roasted Raspberry Chipotle Shrimp Skewers

My friends and I enjoy eating spicy on any given day. This recipe was created with my love for chipotle peppers and some fresh raspberries on hand from the farmers' market. The skewers can be grilled or broiled for convenience. Adjust the chipotle peppers to your heat liking. Recipe comes together quickly for an easy meal. Serve over a bed of rice or Caesar Salad for a light low carb meal.

Serves 4

2 pints fresh raspberries
1 tablespoon stevia or 2 tablespoons white sugar
Skewers, if wood, soak in water for 10 minutes
1 pound large shrimp, peeled and deveined
2 tablespoons olive oil
1 medium shallot, finely chopped
2 cloves garlic, minced
1/4 cup water
1/4 cup honey
Juice of 1 lemon
1/4 cup brown sugar
1 to 2 canned chipotle chiles in adobo sauce
1 to 2 tablespoons adobo sauce
1 teaspoon liquid smoke
1/4 teaspoon salt
2 tablespoons extra virgin olive oil for shrimp skewers

Preheat oven to 450° F. Add raspberries to a large bowl and sprinkle with the sugar. Toss to coat raspberries evenly. Spread raspberries onto a rimmed baking sheet in one layer. Roast for 8 minutes. Watch closely to prevent caramelizing. Skewer the shrimp while raspberries are roasting.

Prepare the sauce. In a medium-sized saucepan, heat olive oil over medium heat. Add the shallot and cook, stirring often until soft, about 1 to 2 minutes. Do not brown the shallots. Add the garlic and cook 30 seconds. Add the remaining ingredients and bring to a boil. Reduce heat to low and simmer 8 to 10 minutes. Transfer the roasted raspberries from the oven and place into the saucepan.

Stir to combine and simmer for 5 minutes, stirring frequently to prevent sticking. Remove the sauce from the heat and purée with an immersion blender or traditional blender until smooth. Set aside.

Brush 2 tablespoons of olive oil over shrimp. Grill the shrimp over medium heat, basting with Roasted Raspberry Chipotle Sauce, and turning. Cook 3 minutes each side.

Marionberry Herb Galette

I'll be honest, I love fresh berries in pie complemented with herbs. Making a pie crust, on the other hand, is not my cup of tea. This recipe was created to have the best of both worlds: An easy-to-make open-face pie full of mouth-watering berries. This fresh berry galette takes the stress out of baking! Three cups of your favorite Rubus berries can make a delightful dessert.

Serves 6

1 pound marionberries, fresh or frozen
Zest of 1 orange
Juice of 1 orange1 tablespoon vanilla
1/2 teaspoon cinnamon
1/4 cup fresh basil leaves, chopped
1/2 cup sugar or 3 1/2 tablespoons Truvia
1 refrigerated pie crust, brought to room temperature (leave in the wrapper)
1 tablespoon cold unsalted butter, cut into pieces
1 egg, beaten

Preheat oven to 425° F. Line a cookie sheet with parchment paper. In a large bowl, gently stir together the marionberries, orange zest, orange juice, vanilla, cinnamon, basil, and sugar.

Unwrap the pie dough, unroll and place on parchment paper. Spoon berry mixture into the center of the dough, leaving a one-inch border. Fold the dough over, making a fluted fold working your way around the pie crust. Brush dough with beaten egg.

Bake for 25 minutes. Remove from oven and let rest 10 minutes. Cut into 6 slices.

Marionberry Herb Galette. *Cooper T. Murray*

Tamara "Cooper" Murray, BA, MA is a graduate of Nazareth College and the University of Kansas. Originally from Binghamton, New York, and living for many years in Colorado, she now calls Alabama her home and enjoys the long growing season of the South. Cooper's influence came from her grandmother who immigrated to the United States and became a cook in New York City for the wealthy. Cooper furthered her culinary knowledge working at country clubs and restaurants. She creates recipes that highlight herbs and has written for numerous magazines and publications.

Cooper's fondness for herbs and cooking led her to develop Organic Herbal Cooking, Inc. Her company offers motivational and educational cooking events in the Southeast. She writes Organic Herbal Cooking's blog and shares the benefits of cooking with herbs in simple healthy cooking. Any conversation with her usually leads to talking about fresh herbs! Not a day goes by that Cooper is not savoring the benefits of cooking with herbs. Contact Cooper at organicherbalcooking.com or coopertmurray@gmail.com.

Anther filaments, wild black raspberries (*Rubus occidentalis*).
Susan Belsinger

Berries for the 4th of July
Diann Nance

It's been a tradition in many Southern families to celebrate the 4th of July with a blackberry cobbler made with the first fruits of the season. Around the first of July, people would start checking out the fence rows for brambles, watching for those little sweet, flavorful wild berries. The challenge was finding enough berries for a cobbler. Occasionally, they had to settle for a pie.

Finding the briar patch was just the beginning. Gathering the berries was full of challenges—thorns, weeds, briars that were not *Rubus*, snakes, and chiggers. So it was necessary to dress for the occasion with long pants, socks to pull over the pant hems, and long-sleeved shirts. Boots or sturdy shoes were a must. Strong sticks for holding back the long, thorny canes to find hidden berries, a bucket for the berries, and a hoe in case of snakes were essential equipment. I have heard of some foragers following John Adams' suggestion for celebrating July 4th with fireworks but not in the way he intended. To ward off varmints before wading into the briar patch, they would throw in some lighted firecrackers.

The reward was always worth it. Whether you pick your own berries or buy them, try the following recipe for berry cobbler on July 4th or anytime. A scoop of Blue Bell homemade vanilla ice cream on top makes it a dish fit for the gods.

Blackberry Cobbler. *Diann Nance*

Double-Crusted Berry Cobbler

Whether you use butter or lard, it is best cold and cut into small pieces.

Makes 12 servings

Crust

4 cups all-purpose flour
2 teaspoons salt
1 teaspoon baking powder
1 1/3 cups butter or lard
1 cup cold water
1 teaspoon red wine vinegar

Process the flour, salt, baking powder, and butter/lard in a large food processor. When flour mixture resembles small, soft beads, add the cold water and red wine vinegar. Continue processing until mixture forms a dough. Remove it from the processor, wrap it in plastic wrap, and place it in the refrigerator for at least an hour.

Filling

4 pounds berries, fresh or frozen
1 1/2 cups sugar
6 tablespoons cornstarch
1 teaspoon almond extract
Pinch of ground nutmeg
1/3 cup butter
1 tablespoon milk
2 teaspoons sugar

Place the berries in a large bowl. In a small bowl, mix together the sugar, cornstarch, almond extract, and nutmeg. Add the sugar mixture to the berries and toss gently.

To make the cobbler: Preheat oven to 425° F. Using about 2/3 of the dough, roll out a rectangle large enough (about 13 x 15-inches) to cover the bottom and sides of an 11x13-inch casserole dish. Pour the berry mixture into the prepared dish. Cut the butter into small pieces and dot the top of the berries.

Roll out the remaining dough to make a top for the cobbler. You may cut a design in the top, or you may want to make a lattice topping. Finish the cobbler by trimming the excess dough from the sides. Brush the milk over the top crust, then sprinkle 2 teaspoons of sugar over the top.

Bake the cobbler at 425° F for 15 minutes, then lower the temperature to 350° F and bake for another hour and 15 minutes or until golden brown. Length of time will vary depending on whether the berries were fresh or frozen.

Pam Trickett

Diann Nance, born and raised on a farm in north central Texas, is presently living and growing herbs among the beautiful rolling hills of north central Tennessee. After a forty-year teaching career which included time spent in Texas, Taiwan, Germany, and finally Tennessee, she realized a long-held dream of starting a plant-growing business, which she pursued for 11 years.

Although Diann is now retired from the business of herbs, she still grows and uses herbs on a regular basis. Her interest in herbs and their uses in our daily lives can be attributed to her mother and grandmother, who loved plants and sharing their knowledge of herbs and plants in general. Diann continues this tradition by growing plants, conducting workshops, and demonstrating the uses of herbs. She is a Master Gardener, a member of the Beachaven Garden Club and The Herb Society of America, past president of The International Herb Association, and a lifelong learner. She may be contacted at dinance40@gmail.com.

Rich *Rubus* Berries: Terra's Transient Treasures

Stephanie Parello

Can you tell I love alliteration? Ever since second-grade, when I learned formally about it and was assigned to write all manner of sentences and stories. Such fun to discover new words and ways to get a point across! Thus began my love affair, also, with the thesaurus.

Back to berries. I love berries, too. The truth is that nothing in our food supply, it seems, is transient or temporary these days. With flash-freezing, what was once only available for a short time in summer can now be had all-year long—without even losing flavor or nutrients. So while we intellectually remember that these treasures are seasonal, go ahead and grab a bag of frozen, if it suits you—and enjoy!

Raspberry/Blackberry Coulis

Coulis is a fancy word for "thick liquid." Actually it means a strained purée, and anything from fruit to vegetables to meat can be a coulis; though, these days, it usually refers to fruit. This sauce will be your new, secret, awesome sauce! It's that little extra something you're often looking for in a drink, a dessert, a salad dressing, or even a protein main dish. I find blackberries are often a bit sweeter than raspberries, so feel free to adjust the amount of honey you use—more or less—to balance what the berries have to offer.

This coulis can also be used to form the base of Raspberry Lemonade (see page 219).

Yields just under 1 cup

1 1/2 cups raspberries and/or blackberries, fresh or frozen
3 tablespoons honey, preferably local raw
Zest of 1 lemon or lime

In a small saucepan, over medium-high heat, place berries. Simmer and stir until berries break down a bit, about 5 minutes. Remove from heat.

Add honey and zest; stir to combine. Purée in a regular blender or using an immersion blender. Then, pass through a fine-mesh strainer.

Pour resultant, silky, smooth deliciousness into a clean jar. Label the jar Coulis and add the date. While this sauce can be kept in the refrigerator for about a month, I've never had it last that long. And if you have quite a bounty, freeze into "ice cubes" for later use.

Raspberry-Basil Balsamic Vinaigrette

Forget store-bought dressing, and make this instead. So good there are no words! See recipe above for Raspberry Coulis.

Yields about 1 1/2 cups

1/2 cup olive oil
1/4 cup balsamic vinegar
1/2 cup Raspberry Coulis
2 tablespoons honey, preferably local raw
1/2 teaspoon Dijon mustard
1/4 cup fresh basil leaves (some upper stem is fine)

Use an immersion blender or place in a regular blender to purée everything together. Pour the thick, luscious dressing into a clean jar. Label the jar Raspberry Vinaigrette and add the date.

This dressing can be kept in the refrigerator for about a month. Note that this glorious emulsion stays together beautifully (that is, it doesn't settle and separate), and will still be thick and delicious next time.

Berries and Ricotta

This is, hands down, one of my favorite desserts using Rubus berries. And honestly, the amounts given in this recipe are my best guestimate, since I never actually measure anything for this one. You can make this just for yourself (a little or a lot) or make separate bowls for each person. Chop the nuts—whatever kind you like—and chocolate chips together, if you're going that route. You can make extra topping and sprinkle it over ice cream another day.

Makes 1 serving

1/4 to 1/2 cup ricotta cheese, preferably fresh
1 to 2 tablespoons local raw honey
3 tablespoons chopped walnuts or pecans
1 to 2 tablespoons chopped chocolate chips
1/2 cup fresh raspberries and/or blackberries
Dash of sea salt

In a dessert dish, spoon in some ricotta; pour honey on top and stir to combine. Sprinkle a layer of nuts and chocolate. Top with berries. Dust with sea salt. Yum!

While always a scientist at heart, and a baker in practice, **Stephanie Parello** has recently begun to take seriously the art of cooking. Herbs and spices certainly hold a high place in this regard, and learning more about them helps food become medicine—or just that much more enjoyable. Stephanie has served on the Board of Directors of the Staten Island Herb Society as well as engages in her own herbal studies, the brewing of remedies, and giving talks and presentations on herbs and crafts.

Path through the blackberry bushes, Middlefield, NY. *Peter Coleman*

Capture Summer Fresh with Blackberries

Stephanie Rose

If you are fortunate enough to gather an abundance of berries, these recipes are a great way to preserve the scrumptious fresh flavor as a year-long treat. Traditional preserving requires a lot of added sugar but by reducing it, or eliminating added sugar altogether, you will get more of the true blackberry flavor packed away in little jars. Here are two low-to-no sugar recipes to enjoy during the cold winter months.

Low-Sugar Blackberry Jam

This low-sugar recipe has half the sugar of berries and—before you say, WHAT!?—yes, that's written correctly. Normally a jam recipe has equal or more of the amount of sugar to fruit, but it results in more of a confection than a fruit spread. The higher fruit ratio also means more fiber and natural pectin to make this jam thick and decadent. It also has the proper ratio of ingredients to be canned and stored in a pantry.

Yields twelve 1/2-cup jars or six 1-cup jars

8 cups fresh blackberries
4 cups sugar
2 tablespoons lemon juice

Lightly rinse the berries and put into a large pot. Crush them with a potato masher or fork. Add sugar and lemon and bring to a boil. Reduce heat to medium low and keep it bubbling lightly until the liquid cooks down to the thickness you desire. I cook mine for 2 to 3 hours, stirring occasionally, to get a really thick final product. This jam will sit piled up on a cracker.

Ladle finished jam into twelve clean, sterilized 125 ml (1/2 cup) canning jars or six 250 ml (1 cup) jars. Process in a boiling water bath for 10 minutes for the small jars and 15 minutes for the large jars. Label and store for up to a year in a cool, dark place.

Low-Sugar Blackberry Jam. *Stephanie Rose*

Sugar-Free Blackberry Jam with Stevia

This recipe is made with liquid stevia to augment the flavor of the natural fruit, but it is truly more of a tart fruit spread than what would be considered "jam." It cannot be safely preserved in a boiling water bath so please keep it refrigerated and use it within a week, or freeze the jars to use throughout the year.

A note about using stevia: Stevia is 200 times sweeter than fruit. Using the glycerite form, I start with two to three droppers full which is roughly a half-teaspoon and taste it before adding more. Sometimes it needs a few more drops, sometimes that is enough. You don't want to go overboard with it or it will add that characteristic bitter taste that people complain about.

Yields six 1/2-cup jars or three 1-cup jars

4 cups fresh wild blackberries
About 1/2 teaspoon liquid stevia
1 tablespoon lemon juice

Lightly rinse the berries and put into a large pot. Crush them with a potato masher or fork. Add lemon juice and bring to a boil. Reduce heat to medium low and keep it bubbling lightly until the liquid cooks down to the thickness you desire.

Continue to crush the berries until the mixture becomes more like a jam, and start adding liquid stevia to taste. Start with just a few full droppers, stir well, and taste. Some berries are sweeter than others so the amount you add can vary quite a bit. Continue adding stevia until it's sweet enough for you.

Ladle finished jam into six clean, sterilized 125 ml (1/2 cup) canning jars or three 250 ml (1 cup) jars. Use within 7 days and freeze what will be stored for later use.

Raspberry leaves are white to silvery-grey on the undersides. *Susan Belsinger*

Stephanie Rose is an award-winning author, instructor, and international speaker who aims to encourage healing and wellness through gardening. For over ten years she has been both a student and teacher of organic gardening, permaculture design, herbalism, and natural skin care formulation. She has written nine books including her latest release *Garden Alchemy: 80 Recipes and Concoctions for Organic Fertilizers, Plant Elixirs, Potting Mixes, Pest Deterrents, and More* (Cool Springs Press, 2020). Stephanie lives in Vancouver, BC, Canada with her family and a motley crew of animals, which provide her with inspiration and delight both in and out of the garden. Stephanie Rose, creator of Garden Therapy® https://gardentherapy.ca.

Shaker Recipes for a Lavish Friday Dinner with *Rubus*

Skye Suter

A blade of grass—a simple flower,
Cull'd from the dewy lea;
These, these shall speak, with touching power,
Of change and health to thee.

- From a Shaker seed and herb catalog,
New Lebanon, New York, 1833

Many recipes created by the Shakers and other past cooks took full advantage of flavors offered by seasonal blackberries and raspberries. Our ancestors enjoyed using fresh or cooked berries and considered wild-collected forms superior to cultivated berries. The juicy berries were added to preserves, desserts, sauces, and other culinary treats. Old-fashioned Shaker recipes include the likes of jam pudding, raspberry sauce, raspberry bread pudding, summer tonics, and more.

Old fashioned flummery was a dessert drink (the modern version being more pudding-like) made with wine, raspberry juice, or other juice, nutmeg, lemon, sugar, and cream. It was often served with a sprig of rosemary.

Another example for an alcoholic concoction, Mixed Berries from a Small Garden, is a recipe that made a huge batch of drink. This recipe called for gallons of water, lots of berry fruits, including blackberries and raspberries, quarts of spirits, plus tartar, pounds of treacle, ginger, and handfuls of sweet herbs with the final result yielding 18 gallons of drink. No doubt it was easier to make large quantities to store away for later use.

The Shakers were not averse to cooking and eating delicious foods. They worked hard all week and looked forward to the Lavish Friday Dinner with four courses, pitchers of a special beverage, and topped off by dessert. This dinner might begin with an herbed potato, apple, or leek soup, followed by a salad of seasonal greens with an herbed dressing, often tarragon. The entrée would be some choice of stuffed seafood, pork, or poultry, often served with a sauce, with two servings of vegetables, anything from creamed corn pudding to string beans to biscuits made from squash. Dessert was often a berry pie, a cake with fruit, or cookies.

The following recipes reflect the four-course Lavish Friday Dinner theme, with beverages and dessert as enjoyed by the Shakers. Every recipe feature *Rubus*, which may be unrealistic when menu planning but typical of eating what's in season. The 2020 Herb of the Year™ can be an impressive addition to culinary dishes of all sorts in all seasons.

Refreshing Raspberry Punch

This delightful summer punch was inspired by a Shaker recipe for a non-alcoholic drink made with vinegar. During certain periods in Shaker history, alcohol was allowed; at other times, it was banned. After a hard week on the fields and gardens, I am sure the members would have found this alcoholic version both refreshing and appealing. Use a less sweet Moscato wine or substitute a Sangria. For a festive occasion, serve in a pretty punch bowl garnished with fresh mint and extra berries.

Makes 12 servings

2 cups fresh raspberries or blackberries
2 bottles (750 ml) Moscato wine
1/8 cup apple cider vinegar, optional
2 cups lemon-lime or raspberry seltzer, or mineral water
Splash of raspberry syrup or Chambord

Place berries in punch bowl or large pitcher. Macerate berries with small amount of the wine, enough to cover, for 10 to 20 minutes. Pour the rest of the wine, vinegar, seltzer, and syrup over the berries and stir to blend.

To serve, fill a wine glass with ice, a few macerated berries, and the finished punch. Top with fresh berries and mint leaves.

Ruby Soup

While not authentically Shaker, this Scandinavian soup is best served cold. Many recipes for raspberry soup call for some dairy product, but this version is made without milk or cream and relies on cornstarch for thickening. Garnish with fresh mint or lemon balm leaves, a dollop of Greek yogurt or sour cream, and/or clementine sections.

Serves 8 to 10

3 cups fresh raspberries and blackberries, or 2 20-ounce packages frozen
3/4 cup orange juice
2 to 3 sprigs fresh thyme
1-inch knob ginger, quartered
1/4 cup sugar or 3 to 4 tablespoons honey
1 tablespoon cornstarch
3/4 cup dry white wine, like a Pinot Grigio or Chardonnay
2 cups fresh berries
Fresh mint, lemon verbena, or lemon thyme leaves

Place 3 cups berries in a blender, puree, then strain to remove seeds. In a medium saucepan, combine strained berries, orange juice, whole sprigs of thyme, ginger, sugar or honey, and cornstarch and blend well. Cook and stir over medium heat until thickened. Remove pan from heat, take out the thyme and ginger, then stir in the wine and additional berries. Chill in refrigerator until ready to use.

To serve, pour chilled soup into bowls, then top with desired garnishes. Serve immediately.

Red, White and Blackberry Salad

Multiple colors in a title create interest in the dish and often give the dish added meaning. Red, white, and blue is a popular color theme for patriotic salads and desserts served around the 4th of July (think of red and blue berries plopped on top of a white cake with white whipped cream.) The blackberries add antioxidants and a dash of color and texture to any dish. Enjoy blackberry as a substitute for blueberry in many such recipes.

Serves 6 to 8

Salad

1/3 cup chopped walnuts, pan roasted and cooled
2 Belgian endives, cut crosswise into circles
1 head radicchio, cut into bite-sized pieces
1 small bunch arugula, chopped
1/2 cup bleu cheese or gorgonzola cheese, crumbled
1 to 1 1/2 cups fresh blackberries or black raspberries

Vinaigrette

2 tablespoons raspberry vinegar, or balsamic vinegar
3 tablespoons extra virgin olive oil
Salt and pepper
2 to 3 sprigs fresh tarragon, leaves stripped and minced
1 to 2 sprigs fresh thyme, leaves stripped and minced

Place chopped walnuts in a small cast iron pan and dry roast for 3 to 4 minutes, then set aside to cool.

In the base of a large bowl, add vinegar, olive oil, salt, pepper and minced herbs. Whisk ingredients to blend. Add the greens and walnuts. Toss to blend, then add bleu cheese and toss again. Top with blackberries and lightly toss. Serve immediately on salad plates.

Piquant Raspberry Sauce

Raspberry sauces are not just for desserts. They add zest and color when served over a main dish, their tartness a nice contrast to fatty meats like pork or duck. Raspberry sauces can enhance everything from tofu to fish. This sauce was adapted from a Shaker recipe.

Makes about 3 cups

2 cups raspberries, fresh or frozen
1/2 cup water
1/2 teaspoon cinnamon
1/4 teaspoon allspice
2 tablespoons raw honey
1/4 cup orange juice
1 tablespoon lemon juice
1 tablespoon cornstarch
1/2 cup water

Crush berries through a plastic colander or sieve lined with a light cloth. Acidic berries should not have contact with metal. Combine strained berries, 1/2 cup water, cinnamon, allspice, honey, and juices in an enamel-coated saucepan. Bring to a boil. Blend cornstarch with 1/2 cup water and stir into the mix. Reduce heat and continue stirring until sauce is clear the desired thickness. Pour over pork chops or hot ham slices just before ready to serve.

Seasonal Vegetables with Hot Raspberry Sauce

Feel free to substitute other seasonal vegetables for the ones listed below. Try carrots, turnips, rutabagas, or other root vegetables. Onions or leeks cut into large chunks, or Brussels sprouts can also be added to or substitute for some of the ingredients below.

Makes 6 to 8 servings

10 ounces parsnips, peeled and cut into bite-sized pieces
6 ounces mushrooms, roughly chopped into bite-sized pieces
1 large acorn or butternut squash, cut into bite-sized pieces
1 tablespoon fresh rosemary, finely chopped
1 tablespoon extra-virgin olive oil
Salt and pepper to taste

Preheat oven to 400° F. In a large bowl, toss vegetables with olive oil, rosemary, salt, and pepper, then lay them on a baking sheet to cook for 30 to 40 minutes. Stir occasionally so they cook evenly. They are ready to come out when fork tender.

Raspberry Sauce

2 tablespoons olive oil
2 jalapeños, diced
2 cloves garlic
2 tablespoons adobo sauce
2 cups fresh raspberries
1/4 cup apple cider vinegar
1/2 teaspoon salt
1/4 cup honey

While vegetables are cooking, prepare the raspberry sauce. Heat olive oil in a saucepan over medium-low heat. Sauté jalapeños in the oil for 3 to 4 minutes. Add minced garlic and adobo sauce and cook for another minute. Add raspberries, vinegar, salt, and honey. Simmer 15 to 20 minutes until reduced by half. Remove from heat, allow to cool slightly, and serve over roasted vegetables.

Apple-Berry Pie with Rosewater

Use your favorite pie crust recipe or a store bought pie crust.

3 to 3 1/2 cups peeled, sliced baking apples
1 cup fresh or partially thawed frozen raspberries
1 tablespoon heavy cream
1 tablespoon rosewater
3/4 cup granulated sugar
1/4 cup flour
1/4 to 1/2 teaspoon ground nutmeg, optional
1/2 teaspoon salt
2 to 4 tablespoons butter
Pastry for two 9-inch crusts
Flour for work surface

Preheat oven to 375° F. In one bowl, combine the apples, raspberries, cream and rosewater. In another bowl, combine the sugar, flour, nutmeg and salt. Sprinkle over the apples and raspberry mixture and set aside.

Prepare pastry and line a pie dish with the bottom crust. Fill this with the apple-raspberry mixture and dot with butter.

Cover with top crust, then flute the edges to seal, making sure to cut a few vents in the crust. Place pie on foil-lined cookie sheet to catch any overflow. Bake for 1 hour and 15 minutes. Edges may be foiled 45 minutes into baking to prevent too much browning.

See bio page 81.

Black raspberry patch, Longwood Gardens, Pennsylvania. *Peter Coleman*

Rubus Tips from the Top of Manhattan

Ann Sprayregen

Upper Manhattan offers many wonderful restaurants and here are recipes from two of my favorite chefs. First, Chef Nicholas Wright brings his farm-to-kitchen culinary vision and skills to the lively and diverse Inwood/Washington Heights population (and visitors from near and far) at the Indian Road Cafe on the banks of Muscota Marsh at the northern tip of Manhattan, where the narrow Harlem River flows between the cliffs of Manhattan and the Bronx to join the waters of the great Hudson.

A few blocks further south, Chefs Jemal Edwards and Brad Doles in their working pastry kitchen shop/cafe, CHOCnyc, are similarly committed to the use of fresh local and seasonal ingredients to create the unique flavors and wonderful variety of sweet and savory baked goods their neighbors have embraced. We are excited to be able to share some thoughts and recipes from these great chefs.

Part I

Chef Nick recalls that raspberry was "the flavor of my childhood." For his birthday, his dad would make him a raspberry pie from the raspberries they picked growing wild around the fields and golf course near their cabin in Brewster, New York. They also made jam. Chef Nick chose the following recipes from his large raspberry file to illustrate the widely differing food items in which this delicious berry can play a major role.

Raspberry BBQ Sauce

Use on your favorite rib recipe, over chicken, fish, roasted vegetables, or as a dip for dumplings.

Makes about 1 1/2 quarts

1 pound fresh or frozen raspberries
1 to 2 teaspoons sugar
4 tablespoons fresh, minced onion or shallots
2 tablespoons smashed garlic, minced
1 teaspoon olive oil
36-ounce bottle ketchup
2 tablespoons spicy Dijon mustard
8-ounce jar honey
1 cup dill pickle juice
1/2 cup brown sugar
1/3 cup sherry vinegar
1 tablespoon red pepper flakes
1 tablespoon fine sea salt
1 tablespoon sriracha sauce

In a glass bowl, mix raspberries with a sprinkling of sugar. Cover and allow to macerate for 2 to 3 hours.

In a large saucepan, brown onion and garlic in olive oil over low heat until evenly caramelized and very dark in color, about 20 minutes. Add raspberry maceration and all other ingredients and bring to a gentle boil. Stir well and remove from heat. Strain through a *tammis* or fine strainer and store in the refrigerator for up to a week. For longer storage, pour into clean canning jars, cover with lids, boil for 10-20 minutes, then store for up to 8 months.

Raspberry Mousse with Almond Cake

You will need 5-ounce round silicone molds to put together this awesome dessert. This recipe calls for making your own jam layer, but feel free to use your own favorite brand if pressed for time.

Makes 6 servings

Mousse

2 sheets gelatin
1/2 cup cold water
1 pound fresh raspberries
3 tablespoons sugar
1 quart heavy cream

Bloom the gelatin in cold water. In a saucepan, boil raspberries, sugar, and a quarter of the cream until broken down. Remove from heat and allow to cool for 1 minute then mix in the gelatin. Blend well, then strain out raspberry solids. Cover tightly with plastic wrap and allow to cool in the refrigerator for a least 6 hours, until very cold.

Mix with remaining cream and whip vigorously for 10 minutes or until soft peaks form. See instructions below.

Raspberry Jam

1/2 pound fresh raspberries
1 cup sugar
1/2 cup lemon juice
Zest of 2 lemons

Boil all ingredients together until blended. Remove from heat, cool and store in the refrigerator until needed.

Almond Cake

3/4 cup plain or Greek yogurt
1 1/2 cups sugar
4 large eggs
1 1/2 cups all-purpose flour
3/4 cup almond flour meal
3 teaspoons baking powder
3/4 teaspoon salt

1 teaspoon almond extract
2 teaspoons vanilla extract
3/4 cup sunflower oil

In a large bowl, mix together all ingredients. Lay dough out onto a greased cookie sheet and bake at 350° F for 5 to 8 minutes until set. Cool then punch out circles big enough to fit snugly into the widest part of your silicone molds.

Almond Crumble

1/2 pound butter
1/4 pound brown sugar
1/4 pound almond flour

In a baking pan, mix all ingredients into a dry crumble. Bake at 350° F until dry, about 10 to 15 minutes. Once cooled, crumble further by hand. Store in a covered container in refrigerator.

To assemble:

Pipe the raspberry mousse into 5-ounce silicone molds. Insert a spoonful of jam into center, then cover with more mousse, leaving a 1/4-inch space at the top. Chill and allow to set for an hour.

Punch out rounds of almond cake to fit snuggly on top of the mousse in the silicon molds, then freeze until solid. Unmold the mousse onto decorative plates and warm a small amount of the jam. Glaze the frozen mousse with the jam, then defrost in refrigerator for 20 minutes.

Decorate with fresh raspberries, almond crumble, and basil or mint leaves.

Part II

In the tiny cafe area of the CHOCnyc bakery in the Inwood section of Upper Manhattan, folks of all ages sip and nibble, watching Chef Jemal Edwards and his crew work on their creations in the larger kitchen area. Meanwhile Chef Brad Doles supervises the apprentices patiently waiting while the line of customers go through the excruciating decision process to select just the right sweet or savory. Chef Jemal has worked as a pastry chef throughout the United States, France, Austria, Italy, and Japan. His pastries and desserts embody the best elements of these cultures and cuisines. Chef Brad, who has had extensive experience in hospitality management with a kitchen background, works closely with Chef Jemal to ensure the promise of consistency and quality in all their products.

Talking about berries often seems to bring back warm childhood memories. Chef Jemal reminisced about summer days in northwestern Louisiana, walking along the railroad tracks with family and friends picking blackberries—the golden sun, rich scents, and sweetness of the berries, laughter, everyone trying to avoid the brambles. Then suddenly he remembered his more recent experience of discovering the low-lying, tiny sweet cloudberries covering the ground in Norway, cherished by the Sami and other reindeer herders.

When asked to contribute to this article, Chef Jemal thoughtfully agreed and decided on one of his notably delicious and attractive confections. He carefully has reworked the recipe to make it user-friendly. For more information, visit chocnyc.com. He uses silicone dome molds that are 2.5-inches in base diameter.

Chocolate Raspberry Tart

Makes four 7-inch tart shells

Chocolate Tart Dough

10 ounces all-purpose flour (300 g)
2 ounces cocoa powder (55 g)
1 teaspoon salt (3 g)
1 pound plus 12 ounces butter (800 g)
3 teaspoons vanilla extract (10 g)
5 ounces sugar (160 g)
3.5 ounces dark brown sugar (100 g)
2 whole eggs

Sift together the all-purpose flour, cocoa powder and salt. In a mixer with the paddle attachment, cream the butter, vanilla extract, sugar, and dark brown sugar mixture until it is very light and fluffy. Add the eggs to the creamed mixture and mix until well incorporated. Add the sifted dry ingredient. Mix until incorporated, but do not overmix. Place the dough in plastic wrap and chill for at least 1 hour.

Vanilla Ganache

15 ounces dark chocolate, preferably 60% (450 g)
11 ounces heavy cream (340 g)
3 ounces corn syrup (85 g)
3/4 ounce sugar (25 g)
6 teaspoons vanilla extract (20 g)

Chop the chocolate into small pieces and place into a medium bowl. If you are using pistols, callets, or chips, chopping is not necessary. In a small saucepot, combine the heavy cream, corn syrup, sugar, and vanilla extract. Bring the cream mixture to a boil and pour over the chocolate. Whisk together until ganache is smooth, completely mixed, and well emulsified. Place plastic wrap directly on the surface of the ganache and hold at room temperature until ready to use.

Note: If you are using the ganache immediately after making it, it will be very fluid and can be poured directly into the tart shell. If you have made the ganache prior to assembling the tart, warm it slightly in a microwave until it is a pourable consistency.

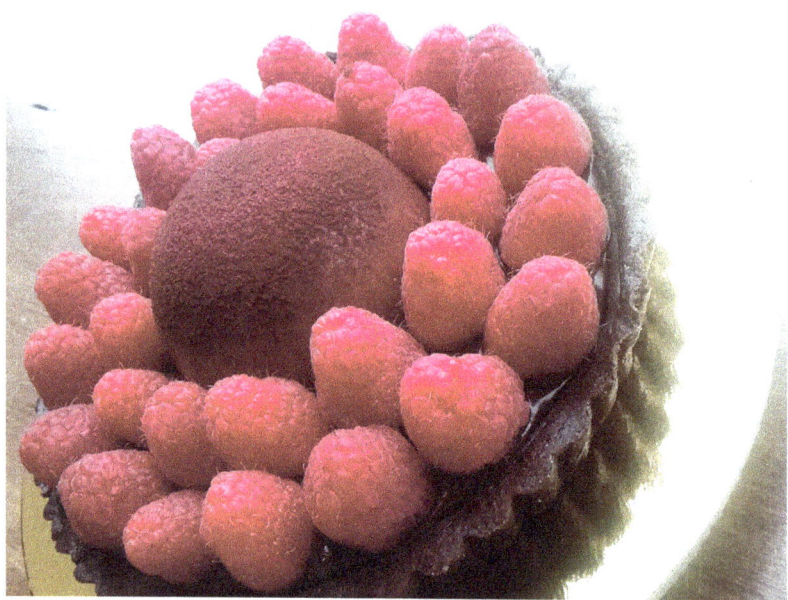

Chocolate Raspberry Tart. *CHOCnyc.*

Chocolate Raspberry Mousse Dome

6 large egg yolks (100 g)
6 teaspoons water (20 g)
3 ounces sugar (85 g)
13 ounces heavy cream (400 g)
5 ounces fresh raspberries (150 g)
1.5 ounces raspberry jam (50 g)
8 ounces dark chocolate, preferably 70% (250 g)
Cocoa powder for dusting

Melt the chocolate and keep in a warm place. In a mixing bowl, combine the fresh raspberries and the raspberry jam. Mix together to combine and to break down the raspberries. Add the heavy cream to the raspberry mixture and, using the whip attachment on the mixer, whip until soft peaks form. Hold in the refrigerator until ready to mix the mousse.

In a mixing bowl, place the pasteurized egg yolks and start whipping on high speed while the sugar cooks. In a small saucepan, combine the water and sugar. Dissolve the sugar over low heat and then cook on high heat until the sugar reaches a temperature of 240° F degrees, then quickly pour it into the egg yolks while they are whipping. Be careful to pour the sugar down the side of the bowl and not into the moving wire whip. Immediately add the melted chocolate to the whipped egg yolks and mix until well combined. This mixture will become a little thick.

Next add half of the raspberry whipped cream to the chocolate-egg mix. This mixture should be mixed vigorously to lighten the chocolate-egg portion, and there are no lumps of pieces of chocolate. Fold remaining raspberry whipped cream into this mixture.

Place the chocolate raspberry mousse into dome molds that are 2.5-inches in base diameter. Freeze for at least 4 hours. Unmold the mousse domes and keep frozen until ready to assemble the tart.

To prepare the tart shell: On a lightly-floured surface, roll the chocolate dough to 1/4-inch thickness. Using a 7-inch fluted tart mold with a removable base, form the dough in the tart shell and freeze for 1 hour. Bake the tart shell at 325° F degrees for approximately 20 minutes. Allow to cool for 30 minutes before using.

To assemble the finished tart: Spread approximately 2 tablespoons of raspberry jam in the bottom of the pre-baked chocolate tart shell. Pour the vanilla ganache into the tart shell until it is full to the top. Allow the ganache-filled chocolate tart to chill in the refrigerator for at least 1 hour.

Just before serving, place a frozen chocolate raspberry mousse dome in the middle of the tart on top of the ganache. Using a small fine tea strainer, sift a small amount of cocoa powder on top of the mousse dome.

Place fresh raspberries around the dome of mousse.

Allow the tart to rest in the refrigerator for 1 hour before serving. Enjoy!

Ann Sprayregen enjoys herbs at restaurants, gardens, and farmers markets. She is Secretary of the International Herb Association Foundation.

Brambleberry resources. *Jane L. Taylor*

Some Brambleberry Adventures for Family, Food, and Fun!

Jane L. Taylor

Some of my earliest childhood memories are of picking wild blackberries (*R. allegheniensis*) and raspberries (*R. idaeus*) along the woodland edges and meadows of rural Connecticut. Juices dripping from my mouth, hands purple (along with a few scratches), and my mother wondering if the stains would wash out of my clothes. But, oh, such was the joy of gathering free fruit. Today's children may only see the berries in the freezer section or in a plastic container so, with the many *Rubus* varieties available, you help bring back some of your childhood, create some memories, and grow some berries.

Children's literature is filled with references to blackberries and raspberries and it is these two berries that will be my focus. Over many years I have been a huge fan of gardens with a theme, and in that context, planning events around a theme. For this focus, I have selected five classics that have stood the test of time. These books are still relevant today and many fun garden and craft projects, activities, and cookbooks accompany them for creative ideas to plan an event. I can speak from experience: garden events focused on a theme can be extremely popular and offer a great opportunity as a fundraiser.

The Latin word *rubus* means bramble. Many of the recipes and activities suggested here can be taken on a picnic to be enjoyed outside on a *bramble ramble,* or foraging garden adventure. In addition, berry picking may give rise to an outdoor adventure as well as an opportunity to have a picnic.

Probably the most famous picnic in all children's literature is that from *The Wind in the Willows* by Kenneth Grahame. Ratty takes Mole for a boat ride along the river, and they unload Ratty's fat wicker basket onto the riverbank. Ratty describes to Mole the basket's contents—thus creating the longest word in English literature.

"There's cold chicken inside it," replied the Rat briefly: coldtonguecoldhamcoldbeefpickledgherkinssaladfrenchrollscresssandwichespottedmeatgingerbeerlemonadesodawater—

"O stop, stop!" cried the Mole in ecstasies. "This is too much!"

Peter Rabbit and friends. *Jane L. Taylor*

The Tales of Peter Rabbit—Beatrix Potter

This first of Beatrix Potter's Tales, *The Tale of Peter Rabbit,* may be the first time a young child hears the word *blackberry*. Potter's words and the stories continue to delight children, and her delicate, botanically accurate drawings always enchant. And so, the tale begins and ends with this juicy *Rubus*.

"Flopsy, Mopsy, and Cotton-tail, who were good little bunnies, went down the lane to gather blackberries...Flopsy, Mopsy, and Cotton-tail had bread and milk and blackberries, for supper."

Brambleberry Cookies

Use this or any sugar cookie recipe that can be rolled and cut into shapes.

Makes 12 cookies

1 cup blackberries
1/2 cup unsalted butter
1/2 cup sugar
1 1/4 cups flour

Press the blackberries through a sieve with the back of a spoon to remove the seeds. Cream the butter and sugar until smooth. Add the pureed berries and stir well. Add the flour and mix well. The dough will be sticky. Wrap in plastic wrap and chill for an hour.

Heat oven to 350° F. Place the dough between 2 sheets of plastic wrap or waxed paper. Roll out to 1/4 inch. Remove wrap and cut into shapes.

Bake for 15 to 20 minutes until golden brown. Cool before decorating.

And More

Bray-Moffatt. *Peter Rabbit and Friends Cookery Book.* Warne, 1994.

Dobrin, Arnold. *Peter Rabbit's Natural Foods Cookbook.* Warne, 1977.

Emerson, Anne. *Peter Rabbit Cookery Book.* Warne, 1982.

Garland, Sarah. *Peter Rabbit's Gardening Book.* Penguin, 1983.

Hallinan, Camilla. *The Ultimate Peter Rabbit.* DK Children's, 2016.

Lane, Margaret. *The Beatrix Potter Country Cook Book.* Warne, 1992.

McDowell, Marta. *Beatrix Potter's Gardening Life: The Plants and Places that Inspired the Classic Children's Tales.* Timber Press, 2013.

Potter, Beatrix. *The Classic Tales of Beatrix Potter.* Warne, 1902-1930, 1994.

Waters, Jennie. *Gardening with Peter Rabbit.* Warne, 1982.

Brambly Hedge Mouse Cookies and Fairy Cakes. *Jane L. Taylor*

Brambly Hedge Series—Jill Barklem

The title tells readers it is about life in the brambly hedge. This exquisite series is an enchantment for the stories and the remarkable illustrations are all botanically correct. The adorable little field mice live in the brambles, or blackberry hedges. The stories follow the four seasons. Several stories describe their trips to the sea and the mountains.

"The cottage always smelled of newly-made bread, fresh cakes and blackberry puddings." ~ *Spring Story*

"They went to the Stump Store to collect...bramble brandy...and all good things needed for the picnic." ~ *Spring Story*

"The Store Stump was warm inside and smelled deliciously of bramble jelly..." ~ *Autumn Story*

"Soon they were all sitting around the table eating hot buttered toast, drinking blackberry leaf tea." ~ *Winter Story*

Brambleberry Fairy Cakes

Makes 12 to 24 fairy cakes or muffins

12 to 24 fresh blackberries or raspberries
1 stick softened butter
1/2 cup sugar
2 large eggs
1 cup self-rising flour
1 level teaspoon baking powder
Additional berries for top of cakes

Heat the oven to 400° F. Place fairy cake paper cases into a 24-hole mini muffin pan, or a 12-hole large pan.

Measure all the ingredients into a large bowl and beat for to 3 minutes until the mixture is well blended and smooth. Place a paper cup in each hole. Place one berry in the bottom of each cup. Fill each cup half-way with the mix. These will rise very high.

Bake for 15 to 20 minutes until the cakes are well risen and golden brown. Lift the paper cases out of the pan and cool on a wire rack. Decorate with a little frosting, enough to hold a fresh berry.

To make field mice-shaped cookies, use the Peter Rabbit Brambleberry Cookie recipe.

And More

Barklem, Jill. *A Visit to Brambly Hedge.* HarperCollins, 2000. (Contains blackberry recipes.)

Barklem, Jill. *The Complete Brambly Hedge.* HarperCollins, 2011.

Barklem, Jill. *A Year in Brambly Hedge.* HarperCollins, 2017. (4 books: The Four Seasons Collection. Each season's cover displays the life cycle of the blackberry.)

Barklem. Jill and Sue Dolman. *The Brambly Hedge Pattern Book.* Philomel Books, 1985.

Web site: bramblyhedge.co.uk

The Secret Garden: Blackberry Fool. *Jane L. Taylor*

The Secret Garden—Frances Hodgson Burnett

Orphaned Mary comes to live with her uncle in a manor house. It's a very mysterious place where she discovers her crippled cousin, Colin, and a walled garden all locked up. Mary and Dickon take care of the garden and it is life-changing for Colin who learns to walk there. The original "gardens are for healing" book.

"...and [Colin] awakened each morning...with a breakfast of home-made bread and fresh butter…and raspberry jam…"

Mary and Dickon enjoyed picnics in their secret garden. Once Dickon found "a little hollow where you could build a sort of tiny oven with stones and roast potatoes and eggs in it."

Fools would be served in the manor house where Mary lived. A fool is an English dessert made by stirring pureed fruit with custard and it dates back to the 16th century.

Blackberry Fool

Feel free to substitute raspberries for the blackberries. Though I prefer to use fresh berries, frozen will work as well.

2 1/2 cups fresh blackberries
1/2 cup sugar, divided into two
1 teaspoon vanilla
1 1/2 cups chilled heavy whipping cream

Mash the berries with a potato masher, a large fork or in a food processor. With a rubber spatula, press the crushed berries through a sieve to remove the seeds. Discard the seeds.

Sprinkle the fruit with 1/4 cup of the sugar and stir. In a separate bowl, mix together the remaining 1/4 cup of sugar, vanilla, and cream. With a whisk or an electric beater, whip the mixture until it makes soft peaks, but not stiff ones. With the spatula, fold the sugared berries into the whipped cream. Taste to see if it's sweet enough. Add more sugar if needed. There should be streaks of white and purple.

Refrigerate for 3 hours. Serve in glass cups or glass bowls. Garnish with fresh berries.

And More

Budayr, Valarie. *A Year in the Secret Garden.* Audrey Press, 2014. (Activities and crafts.)

Burnett, Frances Hodgson. *The Secret Garden.* David R. Godine, 1911, 1989.

Collins, Carolyn Strom and Christina Wyss Eriksson. *Inside the Secret Garden.* HarperCollins, 2001. (Activities, food and craft ideas.)

Colter, Amy. *The Secret Garden Cookbook.* HarperCollins, 1999.

Martin, Judy. *The Secret Garden Notebook: A Gardening Book for Children.* David R. Godine, 1991.

McDowell, Marta. *Frances Hodgson Burnett and the Secret Garden*, Timber Press, 2020.

Taylor, Jane L. *A Secret Garden's Magical Meals.* Michigan Herb Associates, 2000.

The Wind in the Willows: Toad-in-the-Hole and Dragonfly Cookies.
Jane L. Taylor

Wind in Willows—Kenneth Grahame

The four characters in *Wind in the Willows*, Mole, Rat, Badger and Toad, frequently wander through brambles along the riverbank. Food and the savoring of it with these special companions are enjoyed with many references to jams, jellies and preserves.

"…[Ratty] talked of…jams and preserves and the distilling of cordials…"

Rat looked in the pantry "…they found some trifle…"

Toad Hall Trifle

Angel food cake works well here but you can also use pound cake or ladyfingers. If you don't have a trifle dish, you may also fill individual clear glass cups.

Serves 10 to 12

2 3.4-ounce packages instant vanilla pudding mix
4 cups milk

12 ounces angel food cake, cut into pieces
1 cup chopped blackberries
1 cup raspberries
1 cup sliced strawberries or blueberries
12 ounces homemade whipped cream, or Cool Whip

Add pudding mix and milk to a large bowl and make according to package directions. Add about half of the cake pieces to a large trifle dish. Top with about half of the prepared pudding.

Top pudding with about half cup of each kind of berry. Top berries with about half of the whipped cream or cool whip. Repeat layers. Finish off the trifle with additional berries on top. Refrigerate for about 2 to 3 hours until ready to serve.

Toad in the Hole with Jam Toasts

Makes 4 servings

4 slices of bread
1 to 2 tablespoons butter
4 eggs
Raspberry, Blackberry or Brambleberry Jam

Using a cookie cutter shaped like a toad, cut out the center of the slice. Save the cut-out.

In a large frying pan or griddle, melt a bit of butter and place in the bread slices. When the bread is just turning brown, turn it over. Drop an egg into the hole and cook to the doneness you like.

Toast the toad cut-outs. Spread with brambleberry jam. Serve the Toad in the Hole with the jam toasts.

Note: Brambleberry Jam is a mix of blackberries and raspberries; at times strawberries and or blueberries may be added.

To make toad and dragonfly cookies use the Brambleberry Cookie recipe in the Peter Rabbit section.

And More

Boxer, Arabella. *The Wind in the Willows Country Cookbook.* Charles Scribner's Sons, 1983. (Contains blackberry and raspberry recipes.)

Grahame, Kenneth. *The Wind in the Willows: 75th anniversary edition.* Charles Scribner's Sons, 1908, 1983.

Hunt, Peter. *The Making of the Wind in the Willows.* Bodleian Library, 2018.

Taylor, Jane L. *A River-Bankers Picnic.* Michigan Herb Associates, 1999.

Campbell, Di. *The Wind in the Willows Craft Book.* David & Charles, 1992.

Little House on the Prairie: Thumbprint Cookies. *Jane L. Taylor*

The Little House Books—Laura Ingalls Wilder

The beloved series of *The Little House* Books has thrilled readers for ages. The series follows Laura and her family's life from their beginnings in Wisconsin and their travels to Missouri and beyond.

"Blackberries are ripe, and every long, hot afternoon Laura goes with Ma to help pick them. They grow in the brier-patches down in the creek bottom….It is hard, itchy, pokey, sticky work, but every day they bring home pails full of berries to dry in the sun. And every day they eat as many berries as they want. Next winter they will have blackberries to stew."
~ *Little House on the Prairie*

Thumbprint Cookies

Makes 30 cookies

1 3/4 cups all-purpose flour
1/2 teaspoon baking powder
1/2 teaspoon salt
1 1/2 sticks butter, softened
1/2 cup sugar
1 large egg
1 teaspoon vanilla extract
1/3 cup blackberry or raspberry jam for filling cookies

Preheat oven to 350° F. Line two baking sheets with parchment paper. In a large bowl, whisk together flour, baking powder, and salt.

In another bowl, beat butter and sugar until light and fluffy, about 3 minutes. Beat in egg and vanilla, then add dry ingredients in two batches until incorporated.

Using a small cookie scoop, scoop 1-inch balls onto prepared baking sheets. Pat gently to slightly flatten. Press a thumbprint into center of each ball, 1/2" deep. Fill with a small spoonful of jam.

Bake until edges of cookies are golden, 13 to 14 minutes. Cool on baking sheets before serving.

And More

Collins, Carolyn Strom & Christina Eriksson. *The World of Little House.* HarperCollins, 2015. (Activities, food and craft ideas.)

My Little House Crafts Book, HarperCollins, 1995.

McDowell, Marta. *The World of Laura Ingalls Wilder: Frontier Landscapes that Inspired the Little House Books.* Timber Press, 2017.

Walker, Barbara M. *The Little House Cookbook*. Harper, 2018.

Wilder, Laura Ingalls. *The Little House Books* (9 volumes). HarperTrophy, 1932-1971, 1994.

Anne of Green Gables: Raspberry Cordial and Blackberry Syrup.
Jane L. Taylor

Anne of Green Gables—Lucy Maude Montgomery

Anne, an orphan, lives in Prince Edward Island, Canada, with a middle-aged brother and sister who adopted her. She was adopted so she could help on the farm. Anne, a freckled-face redhead, proves to be a bright and very lively girl. The series of books are beloved as we watch Anne grow up. In the first book, it's hilariously remembered when she and her friend Diana drink the raspberry cordial.

"Diana poured herself out a tumblerful, looked at its bright-red hue admiringly, and then sipped it daintily."

Green Gables Raspberry Cordial

2 1/2 cups raspberries
3/4 cup sugar
4 cup water
2 lemons

In pan cook raspberries, sugar and water, until sugar dissolves, about 20 minutes. Pour mixture through a sieve; press with back of spoon. Squeeze lemons and remove any seeds. Add to raspberry juice. Refrigerate before serving.

Blackberry or Raspberry Simple Syrup

1 cup berries
1 cup sugar
1 cup water
1 slice of lemon

In a small saucepan, bring water to a boil, then add sugar, stirring occasionally, until sugar is dissolved, 5 to 10 minutes. Remove saucepan from heat and stir in raspberries. Mash mixture using a potato masher or fork. Let mixture steep for at least 1 hour.

Drain mixture through a fine mesh strainer, pressing raspberry pulp with a spatula to extract as much liquid as possible. Discard solids and store syrup in a sealed container in the refrigerator.

Use the syrup for pancakes, or add to seltzer or soda water. Adults may use in cocktails.

And More

Collins, Carolyn Strom and Christina Wyss Eriksson. *The Anne of Green Gables Treasury.* Viking, 1991. (Activities, food and craft ideas.)

The Anne of Green Gables Christmas Treasury. Viking, 1997. (Activities, food and craft ideas.)

Macdonald, Kate. *The Anne of Green Gables Cookbook.* RacePoint Pub., 2018. (Raspberry cordial recipe.)

Montgomery, Lucy Maud. *Anne of Green Gables.* Puffin, 1908, 2014.

Reid, Catherine. *The Landscapes of Anne of Green Gables.* Timber Press, 2018.

Thimbleberry (*R. parviflorus*) bush in Adirondack Park, NY. *Peter Coleman*

Thimbleberries

For the 47 years we lived in Michigan, it was a treat to visit the Upper Peninsula. There, while driving along the rural roadside, we'd see handmade signs for Thimbleberry Jam, considered a great delicacy. The native thimbleberry, *R. parviflorus,* is a handsome shrub and found mostly in the most northern states. The sparse fruits are small and very fragile, and thus must be made into jam right after picking. We grew one from a small start, and it spread for several feet over the years with white flowers and star-shaped leaves; alas very few berries.

Now in Maine, we are growing *R. odoratus,* called purple-flowering raspberry, or in New England, thimbleberry, a native to the northeast. It is a lovely shrub, with beautiful purple flowers and some berries, and it too spreads. Both thimbleberry varieties lack thorns, a plus for growing them in the ornamental landscape rather than to expect quarts of fruit.

Fun Stuff

Enjoy a "bramble ramble" with some children and be a kid again! For a picnic outside, pick red raspberries. No pail? No problem. Teach the children how to string raspberries on a grass stem to carry them. Then stuff your face and let the juices roll.

Blackberry Ink

White vinegar helps to hold the color and the salt serves as a preservative.

1/2 cup blackberries, fresh or frozen
1/2 teaspoon white vinegar (helps hold the color)
1/2 teaspoon salt (serves as a preservative)

Push the berries through a strainer to make a pulp. Discard the seeds. Keep ink in a small glass jar.

All of the five books featured in this article have been made into films, television series, and are on DVD. Check your library or the internet. Some of the following references may be out of print but check with your librarian or the internet as they are easy to find.

Enjoy *Rubus*, the brambleberries!

References

Brocket, Jane. *Cherry Cake and Ginger Beer.* Hodder & Stoughton, 2008. (Classic treats from kids' literature.)

Burns, Diane L. *Berries, Nuts, and Seeds.* Gareth Stevens Pub., 2000. Ages 7 to 10.

Danks, Fiona and Jo Schofield. *The Wild Year.* Frances Lincoln, 2018. (Instructions for tie-dyeing with blackberries.)

Degen, Bruce. *Jamberry.* HarperCollins, 1983. (A rhyming berry poem for pre-school.)

Hodge, Deborah. *Cooking with Bear: A Story and Recipes from the Forest.* Groundwood Books, 2019. Ages 4 to 7.

Jenkins, Emily and Sophie Blackwell. *A Fine Dessert: Four Centuries, Four Families, One Delicious Treat.* Random House, 2015. (The history of Blackberry Fool. The artist used blackberry ink to paint the endpapers.) Ages 4 to 8.

Nozedar, Adele. *Foraging with Kids.* Nourish, 2018.

Pochocki, Ethel. *Maine Marmalade.* Down East Books, 2004. (A little boy forages for berries and makes jam for the fair. Includes thimbleberries.) Ages 5 and up.

Striniste, Nancy. *Nature Play at Home.* Timber Press, 2019.

Young, Kate, *The Little Library Cookbook: Recipes from Your Favorite Books.* Sterling Epicure, 2017.

Tai, Lolly. *The Magic of Children's Gardens.* Temple University Press, 2017. (Ideas for creating magical spaces.)

Walsh, Alison. *A Literary Tea Party.* Skyhorse Pub, 2018.

Wolf, Rachel Jepson. *Herbal Adventures.* Quarto Pub, 2018.

Yepsen, Roger. *Berries.* W. W. Norton, 2006.

Jane L. Taylor was the Founding Curator of the Michigan 4-H Children's Garden, part of the 17-acre Horticulture Gardens on the Michigan State University campus in East Lansing. She was adjunct faculty in the Horticulture Department at MSU and served on the board of the Michigan Herb Associates for 31 years and during that time was a contributor to the *Michigan Herb Journal.* She was an author and co-author of several MSU Extension publications, magazine and journal articles. In 2000 she received the Jane L. Taylor Award, an eponymous award from the American Horticultural Society. She and her husband Lee received the Nancy Putnam Howard Award for Excellence in Horticulture from the Herb Society of America in 2000, and Marietta College named her Distinguished Alumna-2017. She presented the IHA Otto Richter Memorial Award Lecture in 2015. Following 47 years at MSU, they retired to Cape Elizabeth, Maine.

Jane passed away in October 2019. She will be much missed.

Rubus odoratus (Rubiaceae).
Alice Tangerini, Botany Department, Smithsonian Institution

Drinking Rubus

Wasps enjoying wild blackberry (*Rubus fruticosus*). Susan Belsinger

Will You

Shirley Russak Wachtel

Will you be my tayberry?
This is confusing I must admit.
When first I saw you there among the brambles in the garden
Like the boy next door
The one you never notice
Until one day you catch him looking at you—
Or you at him.
He wooed you with tender words and kisses
And made you feel like something
You had never felt before,
A sweetness in your soul.
But then he raised his voice
And there were arguments.
Only angels are pure, you reasoned.
But still your heart began to break
Just a little.
Yesterday under the brambles,
I found it resting on the tip of a prickly branch.
The tayberry.
And didn't know quite what it was
Whether it would sweeten my tea
Or poison it.
I plucked the cluster, plum red, dew covered, waiting
It seemed all its life
Waiting for my touch.
Not raspberry, a swallow of sugar
Or blackberry, exotic, an enigma.
But something all its own.
Single, unique in this world.
As are we all.
I held it in my hand for many minutes before the tasting.
And so I ask,
Will you be my tayberry?

Pictured here are herbs for Cheers to Your Health tea blend. *Susan Belsinger*

Rubus Infusions
Susan Belsinger

The brambleberries—raspberry, black raspberry, blackberry and the many species and varieties thereof—have been used for centuries, infused and drunk as a beverage. I will not go into the many health benefits that their leaves provide—they are covered in the *Healing Rubus* section—but do check out articles by Daniel Gagnon and Jane Hawley Stevens.

Herbal infusions, or *tisanes*, a lovely French term, are simply herbal leaves and/or flowers steeped in not-quite boiling water. They can be drunk hot after about five minutes of infusing the botanicals, warm after 10 or 15 minutes, or the infusion can be allowed to come to room temperature and be drunk or poured over ice for an iced beverage. I do not keep herbal infusions for more than 24 to 48 hours since the botanicals begin to deteriorate after that amount of time.

Leaves can be harvested from the wild or your own backyard; of course, they should be free of pesticides and pollution, not sprayed or near a highway. Supposedly, leaves gathered in the spring are higher in antioxidants and I can personally attest that if you wait until fall, the leaves are much higher in tannins and more bitter. I would recommend new spring leaves or up until about midsummer is the best time to gather leaves.

Otherwise, you can get dried leaves from local herbalists in your community or from folks that you know and trust. I get dried medicinal herbs from Zack Woods Herb Farm, Hearthsong Herbs, Healing Spirits Herb Farm, Mountain Rose Herbs, Dandelion Botanicals, and Starwest Botanicals.

I have a large stand of wineberries (*R. phoenicolasius*) and they also grow along my driveway, so I gather and dry them to use for my infusions—I dry and keep the leaves whole and crumble them into the pot as needed. They taste more like raspberry leaves to me than blackberry. To my olfactory senses raspberry, wineberry, and blackberry leaves all smell mildly herbaceous with a hint of fruit that is berrylike. The berry aroma is more pronounced in the foliage of raspberry and wineberry than it is in blackberry.

Upon infusing the *Rubus* leaves, the aroma becomes stronger, smelling quite herby, a little sweet, a bit musky and slightly floral with perhaps a hint of chamomile. The first taste of the infusion is herbaceous, rather suggestive of a fermented green tea with just a slight hint of ash, a bit of berry; mild and pleasant, followed by the feeling of tannins on the tongue, mildly astringent. Some might add a little honey to sweeten, though I do not need it.

So let's take some of these *Rubus* leaves and brew a few lovely herbal infusions.

Simply *Rubus*

Use any Rubus leaves or a combination thereof, to make a simple infusion. I use the ratio of about 1 heaping tablespoon of dried leaves or a small handful of fresh leaves for 1 cup of hot water if I am brewing in a cup that has a strainer and lid for infusing. However, I have a two-cup teapot that I use more often since it has more room. I like the infusion best hot; feel free to add a bit of honey if desired.

For 2 cups

2 cups near-boiling water
2 rounded tablespoons raspberry and/or blackberry leaves

Put the kettle on to boil. Just before it whistles and comes to a full boil, pour a bit of water into your pot to warm it, swish it around and discard. Add the bramble leaves and pour the hot water over the leaves to fill the pot. Cover and let steep for about 5 minutes.

Strain the infusion into your cup and sweeten if desired.

Cheers to Your Health

This combination of herbs is great to drink as an afternoon cuppa, after a meal, or before bed. It is both soothing to the tummy and relaxing. It is first redolent of chamomile with a mild citrus scent from the lemon balm, followed by a hint of berries and herbs. The ratio is about 1 scant tablespoon of each herb to a cup of water, which makes a rather strong infusion; use a bit less when making tea in a two- or four-cup teapot.

Makes 2 cups

2 cups near-boiling water
About 1 1/2 tablespoons raspberry leaves
About 1 1/2 tablespoons blackberry leaves
About 1 1/2 tablespoons lemon balm leaves
About 1 1/2 tablespoons chamomile flowers

Put the kettle on to boil. Just before it whistles and comes to a full boil, pour a bit of water into your pot to warm it, swish it around and discard. Add the bramble leaves, lemon balm, and chamomile and pour the hot water over the botanicals to fill the pot. Cover and let steep for about 5 minutes.

Strain the infusion into your cup and sweeten if desired.

Simply *Rubus* Infusion. *Susan Belsinger*

Really Rosy *Rubus* Infusion

This lovely drink is a luscious shade of pink that is brimming with vitamin C, which you can taste with every sip. It has a pleasant aroma of berries and herbs, and a taste of berries first, not big though present, with an herbal finish. I use my four-cup teapot for this infusion because I like it leftover to drink as an iced tea too. I use a combo of both raspberry and blackberry leaves and fruits; however, you can use all raspberry or all blackberry if that is what you have.

If you put your herb leaves in a teaball or strainer, then you can remove it after infusing and when you pour the tea, you'll get some bits of berries in your cup, which is a bonus to munch on when you have finished sipping.

Makes 4 cups

4 cups near-boiling water
1 cup mixed raspberries and blackberries, fresh or frozen;
        lightly crush about half of them
About 3 tablespoons *Rubus* leaves
About 2 tablespoons local, mild-flavored honey

Put the kettle on to boil. Just before it whistles and comes to a full boil, pour a bit of water into your pot to warm it, swish it around and discard. Add the berries and bramble leaves and pour the hot water over the botanicals to fill the pot. Cover and let steep for about 5 minutes.

Add the honey to the pot and stir. Strain the infusion if you have not captured the herbs in a strainer or do not want berries floating in your cup.

See bio page 27.

Really Rosy *Rubus* Infusion. *Susan Belsinger*

Best Berries Smoothie. *Susan Belsinger*

Rubus Smoothies: It's the Berries!
Pat Crocker

Berry Medicine

Who doesn't flip over the red, blue, purple, sometimes orange, and black nuggets of tangy, sunny goodness we love to devour in pies, puddings, cobblers and grunts, sauces, ice cream, tossed over cereal, rolled up in crepes, or slipped into smoothies? Some might claim that no other fruits are more loved or better for you than bright and beautiful berries. One of nature's greatest gifts, the entire patch of *Rubus* offers exceptional phytonutrients packaged in gem-sized thimbles and caps.

According to Doctors James Joseph and Daniel Nadeau, "In the ORAC (Oxygen Radical Absorbance Capacity, or antioxidant, anti-aging measuring capacity) tests at Tufts, black and blue foods neutralized more free radicals than any other foods." Free radicals are unstable bodies that damage healthy cells and blackberries (along with blueberries) were clear winners among fresh fruits in reducing their damage. Indeed, dark-colored berries are nutritional powerhouses due to the intense doses of the antioxidant anthocyanins they contain. Dr. James Joseph, U.S. Department of Agriculture Human Nutrition and Research Center on Aging at Tufts University rates blueberries at the high score of 2400 in ORAC and blackberries at 2036 units of oxygen radical absorbance capacity.

Anthocyanins—from the Greek *anthos*, meaning flower and *kyanos* for dark blue—are nature's sunblock for plants. Along with the orange and yellow pigments, or carotenoids, anthocyanins protect plants from the damaging ultraviolet sunlight. In humans, the antioxidant power of both pigments serves to reduce the oxidative or aging effect of free radicals as they pass through the body ravaging healthy cells. Not only do anthocyanin antioxidants slow the aging process, but also they help fight heart disease, cancer and other modern diseases.

Before scientific study indicated that the juice from fresh or frozen blackberries offers protection against liver disorders, North American native peoples were making a decoction of red raspberry root as a curative eyewash and the Menominee combined the root of black raspberry with Saint John's Wort (*Hypericum ascyron*) to treat consumption (Forsell). Old-time country folk may recall a time when the vitamin C-rich leaves of black raspberries were dried and steeped for a nourishing winter tea.

Whether you forage for evergreen blackberries (*R. lacineatus*) or the highbush variety (*R. allegheniensis*), or you simply add a cultivated crop to your shopping basket, be sure to freeze them in half-cup portions to enjoy all winter.

One of the easiest and most satisfying ways to incorporate *Rubus* and other berries into your daily routine is to add them to smoothies. To get you started, try the following recipes adapted from my book, *The Smoothies Bible* (Robert Rose, 2003, 2010), and drink to your health.

Black Belt Smoothie

Makes 1 serving

3/4 cup freshly squeezed orange juice
1/2 cup fresh or frozen blackberries
1/4 cup fresh or frozen blueberries
4 frozen banana chunks

In a blender, combine orange juice, blackberries, blueberries, and banana. Secure lid and blend from low to high if using a variable speed blender until smooth.

Berry Yogurt Flip Smoothie

*I use cooked fresh or frozen elderberries for this delectable beverage. *Raw elderberries can make many people sick. Cook in a small amount of water, cool and drain.*

Makes 1 serving

1/2 cup cranberry-raspberry juice
1 cup cooked fresh or frozen blueberries or elderberries*
1/2 cup frozen whole açai berries, partially thawed
6 almonds
1/2 cup plain yogurt

In a blender, combine cranberry-raspberry juice, blueberries or elderberries, açai berries, and almonds. Secure lid and blend on low for 30 seconds. Add yogurt and blend on high until smooth.

Best Berries Smoothie

Makes 1 serving

3/4 cup pineapple juice
2 tablespoons freshly squeezed lemon juice
3 tablespoons plain or frozen yogurt
12 fresh or frozen raspberries
1 banana, cut into cubes

In a blender, combine pineapple juice, lemon juice, yogurt, raspberries, and banana. Secure lid and blend from low to high if using a variable speed blender until smooth.

Berry Blast Smoothie

Makes 1 serving

3/4 cup blackberry or raspberry juice
2 tablespoons freshly squeezed lemon juice
1/2 cup fresh or frozen blackberries
1/2 cup fresh or frozen raspberries
6 fresh or frozen strawberries

In a blender, combine blackberry juice, lemon juice, blackberries, raspberries, and strawberries. Secure lid and blend from low to high if using a variable speed blender until smooth.

Berry Bonanza Smoothie

Instead of blueberries, I sometimes use cooked fresh or frozen elderberries for this berry-licious beverage. *Raw elderberries can make many people sick. Cook in a small amount of water, cool and drain.

Makes 1 serving

1/2 cup raspberry or cranberry-raspberry juice
2 tablespoons freshly squeezed lime juice
1/2 cup cooked fresh or frozen elderberries* or blueberries
6 frozen strawberries
1/2 cup fresh or frozen raspberries

In a blender, combine raspberry juice, lime juice, elderberries, strawberries, and raspberries. Secure lid and blend from low to high if using a variable speed blender until smooth.

California Cup Smoothie

Makes 1 serving

1/2 cup raspberry or cranberry-raspberry juice
1/2 cup fresh or frozen loganberries or raspberries
1/2 cup fresh or frozen blackberries
1/2 cup seedless red grapes
1/2 ripe avocado

In a blender, combine raspberry juice, loganberries, blackberries, grapes, and avocado. Secure lid and blend from low to high if using a variable speed blender until smooth.

Black Currant-Blackberry Smoothie

Makes 1 serving

2/3 cup apple juice
1/2 cup fresh or frozen black currants
1 cup fresh or frozen blackberries
1 banana, cut into cubes
1/3 cup plain yogurt
2 tablespoons liquid honey, or to taste

In a blender, combine apple juice, currants, blackberries, banana, yogurt, and honey. Secure lid and blend from low to high if using a variable speed blender until smooth.

Berries and Cream Smoothie

Makes 1 serving

1/2 cup almond or rice milk
1 cup fresh or frozen blackberries
1 cup fresh or frozen blueberries
1/4 cup silken (soft) tofu or frozen yogurt

In a blender, combine almond milk, blackberries, blueberries, yogurt, and tofu. Secure lid and blend from low to high if using a variable speed blender until smooth.

References

Forsell, Mary. *Berries*. Bantam Books, 1989.

https://www.sciencedirect.com/topics/agricultural-and-biological-sciences/rubus

See bio page 106.

Wild green blackberries in central New York. *Peter Coleman*

Eat, drink, and be berry! *Karen England*

Cocktails, Anyone?
Karen England

Berry Classic Cocktails using *Rubus* Species

As I write this piece, I'm struck by how many people, bona fide lifelong horticulturists and the like, on hearing what the 2020 Herb of the Year™ is, have told me that blackberries, raspberries, et al, the *Rubus* species, are not herbs. I am quick to set them straight and thank them for giving me an opportunity to prove why the herb of the year idea is such a valuable herb educational tool. I get to tell them what defines an herb: "a useful plant; useful for cooking, crafting/decoration and/or medicine." Then I am able to add that blackberries and their *Rubus* cousins are all three! A trifecta!

Many start to see right away that the culinary aspect alone makes it an herb by definition but question it being the other two. I ask them if they have ever been given a raspberry leaf tea to drink? Chances are they have—it's full of immune boosting vitamins and nutrients and herbalists have been prescribing it for centuries to treat many ailments. That means it's medicinal.

Two out of three, but, "Come on!" they say. "Used for crafting? For decoration? That third category of use is a stretch." To which I say, "How do you like my perfume?" (and I have never had anyone not like it but they do look perplexed as they answer.) I then reach in my purse and bring out my favorite Jo Malone of London cologne for them to see for themselves what scent I wear—Blackberry & Bay! I believe perfumery is as crafty as soap making and I rest my case.

Everyone knows that blackberries and raspberries and the like are beloved by chefs in the kitchen, but they are also revered by mixologists in the bar, and the Bramble cocktail and its variations make the quintessential aptly named *Rubus* cocktail.

What is a bramble? According to the dictionary, it is a prickly scrambling vine or shrub, especially a blackberry or other wild shrub of the rose family.

However, the *Bramble* cocktail is a1980's British drink hailing originally from the Soho area of London, England. It is a Blackberry-and-Gin-based drink. I make this drink so often in various forms that I have come to think of it more as a drink method than a single drink.

If you make a Bramble cocktail with raspberries instead of the blackberries called for in the recipe, then it is called a *Ramble*. If the Gin in either recipe is swapped out for Scotch Whiskey, it is called a *Dramble*. You see the possibilities. The original drink did not feature other herbs of any kind but the addition of other herbs (in the case of the Bramble, lavender) makes the drink something special and infinitely better than any you could order at a bar. And isn't that what we want? To make mixologists everywhere jealous of our homegrown herbal flavors and our ability to utilize a delicious garden bounty that they can only dream of?

A Word about Gin

Without going into a lengthy historical ramble, gin has come into its own again in the last 20 years and the varying botanicals being used to make wonderful gins, many of which are gluten-free these days, have really blossomed. If a cocktail recipe lists a specific gin, please know that you can use any gin that you like and if you don't like gin, you can use vodka. If you are just learning about gin, I highly recommend starting with the little single shot bottles like the ones that are in a hotel refrigerator mini-bar. A large liquor store chain near me has a huge glass display case with hundreds of little bottles of differing boozes and a dozen of them are different gins. Find a liquor store near you with a good variety of single-serving bottles and get one or two of each gin they offer and a good quality tonic water. Then make yourself and a friend a few Gin and Tonics using the different gins you found. This way you can start to taste the differences and see what flavors you prefer without the expense of buying full-sized bottles to do so. You will be amazed at the flavor differences and it will really help you to make cocktails that highlight the flavors you like best. Botanist is one of my favorite gins but if you can't find it, Beefeater or another London Style Dry Gin is often used for the Bramble recipe in bars.

For an Easy Gin and Tonic, or G&T, as hipsters call it, fill a tall glass with ice and pour on a shot or two of gin, then top off the tall glass with a good quality tonic water. Adding a squeeze of lime is optional. Sip and enjoy.

Bramble

Most folks know raspberries and blackberries, but many Rubus varieties have been cross-bred. The olallieberry, with origins in the Northwest, is a tart hybrid berry created by crossing a loganberry with a youngberry. In the Chinook language, olallie *means* berry. *The boysenberry (R. ursinus) is a cross among the European raspberry, European blackberry, American dewberry, and loganberry. For the lavender, I prefer Sweet Lavender (Lavandula heterophylla) or an English Lavender such as 'Hidcote' or 'Munstead' or French Lavender such as 'Provence' or 'Grosso'. When possible, I use 'Pink Lemonade' lemons but 'Meyer' or 'Eureka' lemons would be fine too. Did you know Blackberry Flower Honey is available online? A great, albeit obvious, choice in this instance for the bramble but not essential.)*

Makes 1 cocktail

9 fresh or frozen blackberries, boysenberries, or olallieberries
2 or 3 fresh or dried sprigs lavender flowers
Juice of half a lemon, plus a strip of lemon peel for garnish
1/2 ounce Crème de Mure /Blackberry Liqueur
    (Homemade, recipe follows, or store-bought)
1/2 ounce Lavender Honey Simple Syrup (recipe follows)
1 1/2 ounce Botanist Gin

Bramble cocktail. *Karen England*

Ramble

Use whatever gin you like, but Nolet's uses raspberries, roses, peaches and juniper along with other "secret" ingredients to make their Silver Gin.

Makes 1 cocktail

9 fresh or frozen raspberries
2 or 3 fresh sprigs of spearmint
Juice of half a lemon, plus a strip of lemon peel for garnish
1/2 ounce Crème de Framboise /Raspberry Liqueur
    (Homemade, recipe follows, or store-bought)
1/2 ounce Spearmint Honey Simple Syrup (recipe follows)
1 1/2 ounces Nolet's Silver Gin

Dramble

Makes 1 cocktail

9 fresh or frozen blackberries of choice
2 or 3 fresh rosemary sprigs
Juice of half a lemon, plus a strip of lemon peel for garnish
1/2 ounce Drambuie, a Scotch whisky-based herbal liqueur
1/2 ounce Rosemary Honey Simple Syrup (recipe follows)
1 1/2 ounce Blended Scotch Whiskey

Method for all three versions

In a Rocks glass (also called an Old Fashioned, Whisky or a Lowball glass), muddle* six of the fresh or frozen berries called for, some of the herb of choice in the fresh squeezed juice of half a lemon. Stir in the liqueur, herbal honey syrup, and gin or Scotch. Top with crushed, cracked or shaved ice. I use an inexpensive Snow-cone machine that I got one summer on sale and it shaves the ice perfectly for cocktails such as Brambles and Mint Juleps.

Garnish with 3 whole berries, lemon peel, herb sprigs, and pansy or viola blossoms if you have them. Serve ice cold!

*A muddler is a mixologist's tool that is either a flat metal disc on the end of a stainless-steel bar-spoon or a wide wooden dowel with a flat end. This tool is used to muddle, or crush, botanicals together in the bottom of a cocktail shaker or drinks glasses.

Homemade Organic Blackberry or Raspberry Liqueur ala' Crème de Mure

The recipes for homemade Berry Liqueurs, Crème de Mûre and Crème de Framboise, that I make, I adapted from those found on the Internet. Do search for recipes and find one that fits with your palate. I prefer making them much less sweet than what's available commercially, and that has guided my recipe choices. If you like really sweet things and syrupy sweet liqueurs, consider adding the larger amount of sugar listed. One reason to make your own blackberry or raspberry liqueur, besides controlling how sweet the tipple is, is that you can make it organic!

4 to 5 cups (approximately 1 1/2 pounds) fresh organic blackberries or
    raspberries, washed
1 750-ml bottle of organic red wine, such as merlot
1.5 to 3 cups organic sugar, to taste
1/2 cup (120ml) good quality organic vodka for blackberry
    or 1 cup brandy for raspberry

In a large bowl, mash the berries of choice with a fork. Stir in the wine. Cover and set aside at room temperature for 2 days.

Pass the berries through a fine strainer into a medium saucepan, pressing to extract as much liquid as possible. Add the sugar and simmer over moderate heat until thick and syrupy, about 15 minutes.

Pour the syrup into a heatproof bowl and cool to room temperature. Stir in the vodka or brandy. Pour the liqueur into clean jars or bottles and refrigerate for up to 2 months. Sterilize your jars for longer storage.

Herbal Honey Simple Syrup

1/2 cup organic sugar
1 tablespoon fresh lavender flowers or 1 teaspoon dried for Bramble
Or a handful fresh or a tablespoon dried spearmint for Ramble
Or a handful fresh or a tablespoon dried rosemary for Dramble
1/2 cup boiling water
1 tablespoon honey

Put the sugar and herb of choice in a heatproof jug such as a Pyrex measuring cup and pour in the boiling water. Stir to dissolve the sugar and cover with a plate or saucer and let cool, steeping the sugar water with the herbs as you would for tea. When cool, strain and discard the herbs and stir in the honey. I make this in small batches so it will be very fresh for making drinks and the Pyrex measuring cup makes pouring the syrup easy. If there is any syrup leftover, it will keep in the refrigerator for a few days.

As a 12 year old working for her family's plant nursery, Sunshine Gardens, in Encinitas, California, **Karen England** never enjoyed the plants. That is, not until she got married, at the age of 30, and started to cook and garden for herself. While making spaghetti sauce she had an epiphany and, the next day, she purchased the herb plants called for in the recipe, went home and planted them. Although she planted them "all wrong"—squashed together like canned sardines in the shade, the herbs adjusted to their surroundings and grew. Better than that, they tasted good! That experience changed Karen's life, sending her on an herbal journey of discovery and made her finally happy to work in such a wonderful family business and industry.

Karen is a graduate of Biola University. She has taken three intensive culinary courses with Darina Allen at the world famous Ballymaloe Cookery School in County Cork, Ireland. In addition, she was chef-in-residence at the Lavender Fields of Valley Center for many years, teaching people from all over the world the delicious flavors of lavender as well as being a popular garden speaker in the Southern California region. She specializes in growing and eating all sorts of herbs but especially lavender, roses, and scented geraniums. Currently Karen is the managing editor for the San Diego Horticultural Society's newsletter. When she and her business partner aren't working on launching Cocktail Bitters Company that will utilize all the herbs she grows.

Wild Blackberry Brandy
Kathryn Mollach

Dottie Aufmuth who owned a liquor store decades ago in Fly Creek, New York, gave me this recipe for making brandy from the blackberries growing wild in Otsego County. Cultivated berries work just as well, but many herbalists believe the wild blackberries have more healing potential.

1 quart wild blackberries
3/4 cup sugar
1 teaspoon whole cloves
1/2 teaspoon whole allspice
2 cups brandy

Mix together in a glass container. Turn or shake every day for four days. Store in a cool dark place for two months. Strain and serve.

Kathryn Mollach owns the Tanner Hill Herb Farm in Cooperstown, New York, whose motto is "A little out of the way, a lot out of the ordinary."

Wild blackberries. *Karen O'Brien*

Drink Your Raspberries: Making Liqueurs and Infused Beverages

Karen O' Brien

Berries in the *Rubus* family are well suited to flavoring beverages. Besides tasting mighty fine, making liqueurs and infused wines is a good way to capture the sweet essence of the fruit for later in the year. Using fresh berries is best, but in a pinch you can substitute frozen. I am including recipes below, but it is really best to experiment and use berries in combination with other herbs to create your own special elixirs!

A Little History

Historically, people have been using plant material in alcoholic beverages for centuries. All of the ancient writers of herbals and medical texts, such as Hippocrates, Galen, and Dioscorides, include detailed information on the way herbal preparations could be used to combat disease, enhance sexuality, restore vigor, and even ward off evil. For generations, people used herbs— roots, leaves, flowers, seeds, fruit, and bark—more as medicine, or restoratives, than as flavoring for food. The medicinal and magical components of plants were believed to be taken up by mediums such as alcohol and vinegar, and imparted to those who used it, either topically or by ingesting it.

Beverages that were fermented (beer, wine, spirits, etc.) yielded a product that could be made ahead and stored satisfactorily. From the beginnings of time, man used herbs to enrich their wines, meads, and beer. A recent article in the *New York Times* disclosed that archaeologists have found evidence that Egyptians were using herbs and resins in wine in 1350 B.C. The chemical analysis of pottery fragments showed traces of savory, blue tansy, and artemisia as well as the possible presence of balm, senna, coriander, germander, mint, sage, and thyme. The Chinese, Egyptians, and Greeks all used crude methods of distillation for creating fortified spirits between 800 and 400 B.C. But distillation was rediscovered by an alchemist and monk named Arnaud de Villeneuvre in the thirteenth century, and he introduced flavored spirits to Europe. No doubt he borrowed from Zosime the Panapolitan who lived in the third century A.D., and who authored a treatise on the art of distillation as practiced by the ancient Egyptians.

Alchemists, at the time of de Villeneuvre, were interested in transmuting base metal into gold, but also in the *le quinte essence*, the phrase which de Villeneuvre gave to the new liquid made by distillation that was perceived to be the water of life, or eau de vie. Monks, in charge of saving bodies as well as souls, took to the distillation of these life-giving waters, believing that God had given them the plants with which they could create the elixir of eternal life. Some of these early concoctions were most likely bitter or vile-tasting, but they were considered medicines, not cocktails. The addition of fruits, spices, and sugars a little later that made the alcohol more palatable, and the discovery by the Dutch that the distillation of wine would also preserve it, gave rise to a new industry—the commercial production of these potent potables.

In the fourteenth century, the drinking of these elixirs became wildly popular, particularly by Catherine de Medici and her court. Often, these elixirs were turned to for their aphrodisiac effect as well as their supposed invigorating and revitalizing properties. By the 1700s, they started to be used for their intoxicating virtues as well as their medicinal virtues. It was not until 1755, however, that the phrase *liqueur* was coined in a pamphlet attributed to a Mr. Poncelet defined as "the alchemy of flavor or smell, or guiding principles for blending easily and at little costs, liqueurs to drink and waters to smell."

Herbal Liqueurs

Many of our liqueurs today, such as Benedictine, Chartreuse, and Anisette, have their origins in the potions devised centuries ago, often by monks. The formulas used are often secret, with some using over 100 herbs in their production. The creation of cordials, herb-infused wines, and the like was a common occurrence as late as the 18th century in homes that had the benefit of a still to create them. Though we, too, could distill our wines and spirits today, it is simpler to use prepared spirits (vodka, wine, brandy) and add those elements that appeal to us. The fun of making liqueurs is experimenting with herbs, fruits, and spices, to create our own *waters of life*.

Steep, Sweeten, Smooth

In the first step, prepared additives (such as flowers, leaves, fruit) are added to alcohol then set aside to rest, or **steep**, imbuing the alcohol with essential oils and the flavor of the herb. Step two requires the addition of a sweetener (usually a sugar syrup). To **sweeten,** the sugar is sometimes added at the same time as step one; other times, it is later in the process. The third step is the aging of the blend, allowing it to **smooth.** It is critical that this portion of the process is not hurried, as the alcohol needs time to mellow and produce a liqueur that is not harsh and acrid. The time can be anywhere from three weeks to nine months. This aging is especially required when using grain alcohol. Using 100 proof vodka is preferable to 80 proof, as it is purer. If you want to use grain alcohol (190 proof!), you need to mix in water as the alcohol is too strong and the resulting liqueur could be harsh. Note: Most liqueurs are nowhere near 85 or 95 proof due to the addition of sugar, water, juices, and other ingredients. Using equal parts of water and grain alcohol will give you 95 proof; 2/3 as much water would be 65. About 2/3 as much water as alcohol is a good rule.

Raspberry Liqueur

This is a great beginner liqueur. Fresh berries are best, but you can use frozen in a pinch. The sweeter the berries, the better the liqueur.

Makes 5 to 6 cups

2 pints red raspberries
1 liter bottle of vodka, 100 proof preferred
1 cup sugar
1 cup water

Place cleaned and dried raspberries into a 2-quart jar with a wide lid. Pour vodka over the berries, cap and set aside for 3 weeks. In three weeks, strain out the raspberries, using a coffee filter. The best way to do this is to use a wide-mouth funnel with a mesh strainer in it, setting the coffee filter into that. Slowly pour the liquid in, letting it drain. Then spoon out the berries and let them sit in the filter until they have been drained of liquid. Do not squeeze or mash the berries as this will cause more sediment. The berries can be eaten or used as a topping for ice cream, cake, etc. But they will be potent!

Put 1 cup sugar into a small saucepan, then add 1 cup water. Bring to a slow boil, stirring to dissolve the sugar. Remove from heat and bring to room temperature, then add to the strained vodka. Shake to mix, then set aside for 2 to 3 weeks. Decant into decorative bottles, if you wish. If any sediment appears, either re-strain with a coffee filter or decant and leave the sediment behind.

NOTE: Other herbs, such as Thai basil, lavender flowers, lemon verbena leaves, etc. can be added to personalize your liqueur. Experiment with different combinations, adding the herbs to the raspberries and proceeding as above.

Two Berry Vodka

The very sweet black raspberries make this a very pleasant and slightly sweet-flavored vodka. I find that no extra sugar is needed, as the berries add quite a bit of sweetness to the vodka.

Makes 4+ cups

1 pint red raspberries
2 pints black raspberries
1 liter bottle of vodka, 100 proof preferred

Place cleaned and dried raspberries into a 2-quart jar with a wide lid. Pour vodka over the berries, cap and set aside for 3 weeks. In three weeks, strain out the raspberries, using a coffee filter. The best way to do this is to use a wide-mouth funnel with a mesh strainer in it, setting the coffee filter into that. Slowly pour the liquid in, letting it drain. Then spoon out the berries and let them sit in the filter until they have been drained of liquid. Do not squeeze or mash the berries as this will cause more sediment. Let sit for two more weeks before using. Serve chilled.

Blackberry Brandy

My grandmother always had a bottle of blackberry brandy on hand for whatever ailed you. A small glass was prescribed for anything from an aching back to a headache to cramps!

Makes 2+ cups

2 pints blackberries
1 pint brandy

Place cleaned and dried blackberries into a quart jar. Cover with brandy. Cap and set aside for 6 weeks. Strain out the blackberries, using a coffee filter. The best way to do this is to use a wide mouthed funnel with a mesh strainer in it, setting the coffee filter into that. Slowly pour the liquid in, letting it drain. Rebottle.

The berries can be used as a topping for ice cream, on pound cake, or over waffles. They will keep a couple of weeks refrigerated.

Kir Royale *Rubus*

A Kir Royale is made with crème de cassis, a liqueur made with black currants, combined with champagne. This elegant version features a Rubus liqueur which makes a wonderful aperitif.

Makes 1 glass

1 tablespoon raspberry liqueur (recipe above)
4 ounces champagne

In a champagne flute, drizzle one tablespoon of raspberry liqueur. Add 4 ounces of chilled champagne. Skol!

Peach Melba-Raspberry Sangria

Light, colorful drink for those hot, summer days.

Makes about 10 to 12 cups of punch

3 cups fruit—a mix of fresh peaches, diced, and raspberries
2/3 cup sugar
Floral ice wreath (recipe below)
1.5 liter dry white wine (Pinot Grigio, Sauvignon Blanc, etc.)
1/2 cup brandy
1/4 cup Triple Sec
1 1/2 cups club soda

Stir fruit and sugar into punchbowl and let stand about 15 to 30 minutes. Place ice wreath into bowl, stir in wine, brandy, and Triple Sec. Add club soda just before serving.

Floral Ice Wreath

Great for that summer punch bowl or as a decorative element for chilling salads, etc.

Lemon verbena leaves
Anise hyssop flower spikes
Lavender flower spikes
Assorted edible flowers, as available
Water, tea, juice, or lemonade
Raspberries or blackberries

Using a bundt pan, layer lemon verbena leaves, anise hyssop flowers, and lavender flowers. Fill pan one third with either water or the base ingredient for your punch—such as tea, lemonade, juice, etc. Freeze until solid, then add another one third more liquid with a handful of berries and freeze again. For an even more festive look, add more edible flowers such as Johnny jump-ups, rosebuds, or pinks. If you want more citrus flavor, add some sliced limes, lemon balm leaves, and so on.

When ready to use, float in your punch bowl or use a wreath (water only) as a chilling base for salad bowls.

Raspberry Shrub

One of the drinks we made when I worked at Old Sturbridge Village (a recreation of 1830s life in New England) was Raspberry Shrub. We called it the Gatorade of the 1830s, as it was used during the hot summer haying season to quench thirst. It sounds pretty awful to today's palates, as it is a vinegar-based drink, but it is tasty. We used the recipe from Lydia Maria Child's book, *The American Frugal Housewife:*

"Raspberry shrub mixed with water is a pure delicious drink for summer; and good in a country where raspberries are abundant, it is good economy to make it instead of Port and Catalonia wine. Put raspberries in a pan and scarcely cover them with strong vinegar. Add a pint of sugar to a pint of juice; (of this you can judge by first trying your pan to see how much it holds) scald it, skim it, and bottle it when cold."

Today, you can make this very easily. Place raspberries in a wide mouth jar, and cover with good apple cider vinegar. Let sit for a few days. If you wish to hurry it along, you can place the raspberries and vinegar in a pan and simmer gently for 15 minutes. Strain; keep the liquid and discard the spent fruit. Measure the amount of liquid you have and add it to a large pan. For each cup of liquid add an equal amount of sugar, or half as much honey. Stir well and bring to a gentle boil. Skim it if necessary. Pour into bottles or jars and store in a cool pantry or cupboard until needed.

TO USE: Stir 2 to 4 tablespoons of shrub concentrate into a large glass of cold or sparkling water. More or less may be added to taste.

Blackberry 'Baby Cakes' in flower. *Pat Kenny*

References

Bellis, Ren. *Making Inexpensive Liqueurs.* Amateur Winemaker Publications, Ltd., 1982.

Child, Lydia Maria. *The American Frugal Housewife.* Chapman Billies, Inc. (Reprint).

Cocconi, Emilio. *Liqueurs for All Season.* Lyceum Books, 1975.

Crosby, Nancy and Sue Kenny. *Kitchen Cordials.* Crosby & Baker Books, 1997.

Farrell, John P. *Making Cordials and Liqueurs at Home.* Harper & Row, 1974.

Gulling, Rich and Pattie Vargas. *Cordials from Your Kitchen.* Storey, 1997.

Jagendorf, M.A. *Folk Wines, Cordials, and Brandies.* Vanguard Press, 1963.

Kibbey, Heather and Cheryl Long. *Classic Liqueurs: The Art of Making and Cooking with Liqueurs.* Culinary Arts Ltd, 1990.

Meilach, Dona and Mel. *Homemade Liqueurs.* Contemporary Books, Inc, 1979.

Karen O'Brien, owner of The Green Woman's Garden in Richmond, New Hampshire, is now investigating the possibilities of gardening in the woods, as well as the fields. She hopes that any and all mistakes of gardening past will stay past, and anxiously anticipates new adventures in the hills of New Hampshire. She has unusual herb plants for sale, including medicinal and native herbs, runs workshops on various herbal adventures, and occasionally participates at farmers' markets and fairs. Karen lectures and presents workshops on all aspects of herbs and gardening. She is the Past Botany and Horticulture Chair of The Herb Society of America, is the District Chair of The New England Unit of H.S.A., is Secretary of the International Herb Association, and is Past President of the Greenleaf Garden Club of Milford. She is a regular contributing author to IHA Herb of the Year™ books, and past editor of *Elderberry*, *Savory*, *Artemisia*, and *Capsicum*.

Left-hand—elbow-length gauntlet glove for holding back prickly canes; right-hand—shorter-length, thin rubber glove for actual picking of berries.
Susan Belsinger

Rubus adds flavor, color and nutrition to many infusions: shrubs, cordials and vinegars. *Susan Belsinger*

Bracing *Rubus* Beverages
Stephanie Parello

Raspberry Bay Lemonade

First make some bay simple syrup (recipe below). Other herbal syrups can be substituted—think lemon verbena, mint, basil, or rosemary, but I love bay syrup the most. You can use dry bay leaves, but the taste and aroma of fresh bay leaves are an absolute must for me in this recipe. Then use the berry coulis (See page 141 for recipe), or concentrate, which can be frozen for another time (perhaps to bring a taste of summer into another season) or used right away.

Makes about 2 quarts

Bay Simple Syrup

Yields 1 1/2 cups

1 cup sugar
1 cup water
5 to 7 fresh bay leaves (depends on leaf size and desired strength)

In a small saucepan, over medium-high heat, place sugar and water. Simmer and stir until sugar completely dissolves. Add bay leaves, and continue to simmer for 5 to 10 minutes (depending on desired strength, you could go even longer).

Remove from heat and allow to cool. Remove the leaves and discard. Pour the infusion through a fine-mesh strainer into a clean jar. Label the jar Bay Syrup and the date. This syrup can be kept in the refrigerator for about a month, of frozen for up to nine months.

Raspberry Lemonade

1 1/2 cups lemon juice
1 cup bay syrup
1/2 cup raspberry coulis
4 cups water, sparkling or still
Lemon, thinly sliced
Fresh raspberries
Fresh bay leaves
Ice

Combine lemon juice, bay syrup, and raspberry coulis, and stir well. This is your concentrate. Freeze in an appropriate container, label and date it, or continue to make lemonade.

Pour concentrate and water into large pitcher and stir gently. Taste for strength—I like it fairly strong—if too strong, add a bit more water. Garnish with lemon slices, fresh raspberries, and a bay leaf, if desired. Serve over ice, and enjoy!

Blackberry Bracer

A delightful beverage as is, though a bit of bourbon or rum would not go amiss.

Makes 2 servings

1/4 cup blackberry purée
2 tablespoons orange juice
1 teaspoon apple cider vinegar
1 cup ginger beer
Crushed ice

Combine the berry purée, orange juice, and apple cider vinegar in a pitcher or cocktail shaker and stir well. Add ginger beer and stir gently. Serve over crushed ice, and enjoy!

See bio page 143.

Berry Garden Mixology
Stephanie Rose

Wild Blackberry Cordial

As a term, cordial has many meanings, but this cordial is a non-alcoholic fruit syrup that is delicious when added to beverages. This recipe extracts the unique blackberry flavor into a concentrated syrup that can be added to fancy cocktails or simple sparkling water.

Yields 4 cups

4 cups blackberries
2 cups sugar
2 cups water

In a large stock pot, add berries one layer at a time and crush them with a potato masher. Add the sugar once all berries are mashed, stir, and set on high heat until mixture boils. Add water to achieve the consistency of a thick soup. Reduce the heat to low and simmer until seeds start to separate from the fruit, stirring occasionally. Using a fine meshed sieve, strain out the seeds and discard. Ladle finished cordial into canning jars and store in the fridge for up to two weeks.

To serve, pour 1/2 cup cold cordial into 1 1/2 cups of cold sparkling water over ice or add to garden cocktails. Blackberry cordial is a wonderful addition to a mojito!

Blackberrycello

Blackberrycello is a play on Limoncello, the tasty Italian treat of lemon rind oil infused into alcohol and sweetened with simple syrup. Using a similar idea of combining blackberry-infused vodka and simple syrup makes a blackberry-flavored liqueur that you can store and serve for those perfectly fancy occasions. This recipe takes several weeks to infuse the blackberry and alcohol into a liqueur, but it's certainly worth the wait.

Yields 8 cups cordial

3 cups fresh blackberries
4 cups vodka
3 cups sugar
3 1/2 cups water

First, in a large mason jar with a lid, add blackberries and pour vodka oven them to macerate. For this recipe, an inexpensive vodka will work fine. Infuse the blackberries in the vodka for a week; leave it in a cool dark place.

The next week, create a simple syrup by adding both the sugar and water in a tall-sided saucepan and bringing it to a boil. Stir until the sugar is dissolved and the syrup has reduced to 3 cups.

Allow the syrup to fully cool, then add it to the vodka and berries and allow the mixture to combine overnight. The next day, strain the liquid into a bottle and allow flavors to blend for a few more weeks before serving. Store the finished blackberrycello in the freezer so it's ice cold when you are ready to make cocktails or serve directly over ice.

See bio on page 148.

Manhattan Berry Mixology
Chef Nick Wright

Smoky Raspberry Margarita

Two days ahead, mix a liter of blanco tequila with a liter of good quality smoky mescal. Add 7 ounces of chopped fresh jalapeños and allow to infuse for 48 hours. Strain. You can rim the glass with regular salt, but using kombu-sea salt makes the beverage even more special. To make it, blend equal parts kombu and sea salt in blender until well mixed but still coarse. Found at health food stores and many online sites, the seaweed kombu is edible kelp widely eaten in East Asia. It may also be referred to as dasima or haidai.

Makes 1 serving

1 ounce jalapeño-infused mescal-tequila blend
2 ounces raspberries or raspberry liqueur
1 ounce Patron Citronge
1/2 ounce lime juice

Rim a double old-fashioned glass halfway with kombu-sea salt. Combine ingredients with ice in a cocktail shaker and shake. Strain into glass and enjoy!

Healing Rubus

Branch of wineberry leaves. *Susan Belsinger*

Ode to Blackberries

Gert Coleman

Juicy berries, drupelets with seeds,
delicious in jelly, jam, cordial and wine.
Look for the seedless ones
for cakes, muffins and pies.
Those seeds are hard to chew.
Pick them, buy them, but eat them fast.
They don't last long,
subject to mold, softness, or drying out.

There's more to you, Blackberry, though
than just juice or juiciness.
Those long arching canes
with vicious recurving thorns are
sharp enough to prick your finger,
tear your skin and clothes, blind your eyes.

Your canes offer protection to animals, birds, and insects.
In less enlightened times they offered healing
to the sick, the lame, the infected.
Nine times they had to crawl
beneath your brambly arches,
chanting charms for healing.
Or were carried or passed through by caring hands.

Blackberry, you teach us about borders.
A great forest of brambles arose
to protect Sleeping Beauty until her Prince came.
Nosy neighbors will surely give you a wide berth–
unless contradictorily you are sporting those
juicy purple-black berries.
And then who can resist reaching into
that prickly tangle for the ripest, juiciest of blackberries?
Ouch!

Red raspberry bushes in native food gardens outside Quebec Parliament.
Gert Coleman

Herbal educator, **Gert Coleman** writes odes to herbs in a variety of forms. Loving the outdoors, she walks the hills in Central New York and, with her husband Peter, tends and expands their gardens every year. She teaches nature writing classes as well as herbal discovery workshops.

Natural Beauty with *Rubus*

Janice Cox

Rubus, you are beautiful! I love you berry much!

Growing up in Oregon, picking fresh berries was a simple pleasure my family enjoyed year round. Everyone has a favorite berry patch. It may be a small part of your yard or a secret spot out in the wild or near a country road. My father was a farmer so we always had lots of berries growing near the irrigation ditches and fence lines. They acted as a natural barbed wire.

We would use the blackberries, raspberries, and salmonberries (*Rubus spectabilis*) that we picked in a variety of ways. Of course, eating them fresh after a day of berry picking is best, but you can also create wonderful pies, cobblers, jams, and drinks with the fresh fruit. As a health and beauty writer, I have also come to love these fresh berries as powerful ingredients for healthy skin and hair.

Rubus is a large, diverse group of plants and part of the rose family (another one of my favorites!). The plants are easily identified by their brambles, woody stems, and edible berries. Fresh *Rubus* berries are some of nature's best sources of healthy vitamins and antioxidants. Antioxidants are important for healthy skin and hair because they fight free radicals that age our skin and also have skin-calming, anti-inflammatory properties.

Fresh or frozen berries can be used to cleanse and soften your skin in facial masks and cleansers. The fresh or dried leaves of the plant can be brewed up into a cleansing and refreshing tonic that will keep you healthy head to toe, from a dandruff-fighting hair treatment to a mouth-friendly rinse. *Rubus* leaves and berries are powerful natural beauty ingredients.

I am so pleased to celebrate this useful plant as Herb of the Year™ 2020. Here are some recipes for you to try at home.

Blackberry Antioxidant Facial Mask

Blackberries are known for their great health benefits. They are a source of natural fiber and contain vitamins A, C, and E. Like other berries they are also a rich source of antioxidants. Used as a facial mask, fresh or frozen berries will deeply cleanse and soothe your complexion giving it a radiant glow. Use a fresh berry mask every two weeks for clean and healthy skin.

Yield: 2 ounces, enough for 1 application

2 tablespoons fresh or frozen blackberries
1 tablespoon plain yogurt
1 tablespoon lemon juice

Mash or blend the blackberries together with the yogurt and lemon juice.

To use: After cleansing, spread the entire mixture over your face and neck, avoiding the delicate areas around your eyes and mouth. Leave on for 15 minutes, then rinse well with warm water and pat your skin dry.

Raspberry Leaf Astringent

Raspberry leaves are rich in vitamins B and C and a number of minerals, including potassium, magnesium, zinc, and iron. They also have high antioxidant properties. Raspberry leaf tea is a popular health tonic for this reason. You can find dried leaves sold in bulk at many natural food stores or let your own fresh leaves dry for a few days. This astringent is especially good for oily skin because it is a bit more acidic and drying and will also help restore your skin's natural pH level.

Yield: 4 ounces

2 tablespoons dried raspberry leaves or 1/3 cup fresh leaves
1/4 cup apple cider vinegar
1/4 cup rose water or distilled water

Place the raspberry leaves and vinegar in a glass or ceramic bowl and let sit overnight. In the morning, strain the mixture and discard the leaves. Add the rose water to the vinegar solution and stir. Pour into a clean bottle with a tight-fitting lid. Keeps up to a month at room temperature.

To use: Apply to your skin using a clean cotton ball, after cleansing. Then splash with cool water and pat your skin dry.

Fresh Berry Cleanser

Fresh berries contain anthocyanins, a natural chemical in plants that helps reduce inflammation. Blackberries, raspberries, and dewberries also contain alpha hydroxyl acids that are the same key ingredient in many over-the-counter acne skin care products. This recipe is for a gentle cleanser that will help exfoliate dead skin cells and surface debris, leaving you with a clearer, smoother complexion.

Yield: 3 to 4 applications

2 tablespoons fresh or frozen berries of your choice
1 tablespoon light oil such as almond, jojoba or sesame
3 tablespoons witch hazel

Place all ingredients in a blender or food processor and blend until smooth. Pour into a clean jar and cover. You will want to store this cleanser in the refrigerator because it contains real berries. It should keep for a week or two. If you feel the cleanser has gone bad, it is always best to create a new batch.

To use: Use in place of soap to clean your skin. Apply gently to skin and wash off with cool water.

Rubus Leaf Mouth Rinse

Fresh berry leaves such as blackberry or raspberry make an effective mouthwash with antiseptic properties. This recipe is perfect for those who do not wish to use alcohol but want a clean, fresh mouth. It is as easy to make as a cup of tea.

Yield: 8 ounces

1/4 cup fresh *Rubus* leaves, chopped or 2 tablespoons dried leaves
1 cup boiling water
2 teaspoons fresh lemon juice

Place the leaves in a ceramic or glass bowl and pour the boiling water over them. Let sit until completely cool. Strain off the liquid and discard the leaves. Add the lemon juice and stir well. Store this mouthwash in the refrigerator. It should keep for one week.

To use: Pour about 4 teaspoons into a small glass and rinse your mouth for 30 seconds.

Blackberry Leaf Hair Rinse

Blackberries make a wonderful addition to facial masks and can also be used as a mild dye for dark hair types. The green prickly leaves make a cleansing hair rinse that is a good cure for dandruff and will leave your hair clean and shiny. If you cannot find fresh blackberry leaves, look for dried leaves in the bulk bin of your local natural food store. You can also use herbal tea that is made from 100% blackberry leaves.

Yield: 12 ounces, or 1 application

1/2 cup clean fresh blackberry leaves or 1/4 cup dried leaves
2 cups water

Place the leaves in a small saucepan and cover with water. Bring the water to a boil over medium heat. Lower the heat and simmer for 15 minutes. Remove the pan from the stove and allow to cool for 20 minutes. Strain the liquid and pour into a clean bottle with a tight fitting lid. You will have a mild yellow-green liquid with a mild berry scent.

To use: Use as a final rinse after shampooing. For a hint of natural color add a few fresh berries to water before heating. Be aware that, like any colorful natural product, berries may stain counters or towels.

Simple Berry Lip Gloss

Fresh berry juice can be used to tint lip stains, products that give your lips a natural tint. It can also be used as a natural coloring for bath salts and soaks. You can create a simple and sweet natural lip gloss using all-natural coconut oil and your favorite *Rubus* berry.

Yield: .5 ounces

1 teaspoon fresh berry juice
2 teaspoons coconut oil

In a small glass bowl or container mix together the juice and oil until smooth and creamy. Spoon into a small container with a tight-fitting lid. Stored out of the sun, it will keep for at least a month.

To use: Spread on your lips for a bit of color and protection from sun and wind.

A Note on Foraging and Hunting

I feel I should write a brief "safety" note on gathering your berries and leaves because *Rubus* is often gathered in the wild. Foraging and hunting for wild leaves and berries is definitely part of the fun, but if this is a new activity for you, make sure you check a local plant guide, and/or even take a class from an expert in your area so you know what to look for.

A good rule of thumb when gathering wild plants is, if it is safe to eat, it is usually safe to use on your skin and hair. As with any new ingredient, do a patch test inside your arm or behind your leg before spreading on your face or body. This will avoid some embarrassment and discomfort.

Finally, to harvest responsibly, make sure you have the property owner's permission and bring the proper tools for the job. Most people are happy to have you trim their *Rubus* canes and brambles as they can get out of hand. If you are cutting in a public area, make sure you also check that the berries and leaves have not been sprayed. You do not want harmful chemicals in your body care products.

Be sure to check a guide book when foraging for wild raspberry leaves.
Peter Coleman

Janice Cox is an expert on the topic of natural beauty and making your own body care products using simple kitchen and garden ingredients. She is the author of three bestselling books on the topic: *Natural Beauty at Home*; *Natural Beauty for All Seasons*; and *Natural Beauty from the Garden*. She is the beauty editor for *Herb Quarterly Magazine* and a regular contributor to several herbal and lifestyle magazines. Janice is currently a speaker with *Mother Earth News Magazine* at their fairs across the country. She lives in Medford, Oregon, with her husband. She just became a grandmother and loves teaching her granddaughter the names of all the herbs and flowers growing in her garden. For more information you can visit her website at www.JaniceCox.com.

The Medicinal Uses of Raspberry (*Rubus idaeus*, et al.) and Blackberry (*Rubus fruticosus*, et al.) [Rosaceae]

Daniel Gagnon, Medical Herbalist RH (AHG)

Synonyms: Raspberry: red raspberry, American raspberry, European raspberry

Blackberry: bramble, shrubby blackberry, cut-leaf blackberry

Parts Used: Leaf, root, fruit. Although all three parts of both herbs are used, medicinally the leaves are by far the most commonly used in the United States.

Constituents: The main constituents of these two herbs include: 4% to 15% hydrolysable tannins (gallotannins); ellagitannins; hydroquinone; arbutin; plant acids (including succinic, oxalic, malic, lactic, citric, and isocitric acids); flavonoids; pentacyclic triterpene acids, and traces of essential oils. There are also appreciable amounts of vitamins and minerals in both fruits (Van Hellement 1986, Wichtl 1994, Kurschmann 1996).

Key Indications

Internally: Raspberry and/or blackberry leaves are used to strengthen the uterus during pregnancy and are considered an excellent gynecological tonic (McQuade-Crawford 1998). They stimulate the production and maintenance of breast milk; aid in returning the uterus to normal after delivery; tone the female reproductive organs; reduce or stop prolonged or heavy menstrual bleeding; act as a general uterine tonic following surgery to the uterus, the removal of fibroids, the termination of pregnancy, or following a curettage; stimulate mineral absorption from the gastrointestinal tract; relieve urethral

Wild raspberry leaves have been gathered since ancient times for a host of ailments. *Susan Belsinger*

irritation; and soothe the kidneys, urinary tract and ducts (Bone 2003, Skenderi 2003).

The root of both herbs (although it is easier to get blackberry root commercially) is useful in diarrhea, dysentery, cholera, stomach complaints of children, gastritis, esophagitis, enteritis, irritable bowel disorders, indigestion, tonsillitis, sore throats, and mouth ulcerations.

Additionally, all parts of these two herbs possess significant anticancer properties.

Externally: The decoction of the leaf or root is used as a wash for skin wounds or burns, sores, boils, eczema, psoriasis, raw skin surfaces, chronic skin conditions, skin ulcerations, or hemorrhoids (Bone 2003, Ashok 2012).

A Quick History of Their Uses

A quick overview of the history of raspberry and blackberry use shows that these two herbs have been an integral part of herbal medicine for a very long time.

Theophrastus (300 BCE), a Greek native of Eresos in Lesbos, is often considered to be the Father of Botany. Two of his works, *Enquiry into Plants* (*Historia Plantarum*) and *On the Causes of Plants,* were critically important botanical medicine texts with major influences on Renaissance science (Fournier 1948). He wrote about blackberry and recommended its use as a medicinal plant.

Dioscorides (100 CE), a Greek physician in the Roman army, pharmacologist, and botanist, wrote *De Materia Medica*, a pharmacopeia of medicinal plants and the medicines that can be made from them. His five-volume set was widely read and studied for over 1,500 years until it was supplanted by revised herbals during the Renaissance. In his magnum opus *De Materia Medica*, Dioscorides expounds the astringent properties of blackberry: "The decoction of the branches tightens the intestines and uterus. Chewing the leaves tones the gums. The crushed leaves are applied on skin ulcers and hemorrhoids to heal them as well as on the epigastrium (upper part of the stomach) to calm stomach pains" (Fournier 1948).

In 1633, the Englishman Thomas Johnson edited John Gerard's classic book *The Herbal* (Woodward 1927). Under the heading "Of the Bramble or black-Berry bush", Johnson wrote about the use of the astringent virtues of this herb: "The leaves of the Bramble boiled in water, with honey, allum, and a little white wine added thereto, makes a most excellent lotion or washing water, to heal the sores in the mouth, the priuie parts of man and woman, and the same decoction fasneth the teeth." Johnson also described and commented about the *raspis* or *framboise* (French name for raspberry): "The Raspis is thought to be like the Bramble in temperament and vertues, but not such so much binding or drying" (Gerard 1975, p. 1274).

In 1817, an American botanist W.P.C. Barton wrote about blackberry. He stated that "few native articles possess a greater share of the favouritism of domestic practitioners; and in many sections of our country, blackberry tea [generally made from the root] is resorted to as a general corrective of all vitiated humours, a strengthener of the stomach and bowels, in short a perfect panacea" (Crellin 1990). Barton felt that the claims were overrated, but, in his opinion, there was enough credible testimony to suggest that the herb would be valuable for disorders needing astringent medicine (Crellin 1990).

Wimpy or Nourishing Medicine?

In the early 1980s, as I traveled throughout the United States lecturing about the medicinal properties of herbs, I would talk about the difference between heroic (strong) medicinal herbs such as goldenseal (*Hydrastis canadensis*) root, osha (*Ligusticum porteri*) root, andrographis (*Andrographis paniculata*) herb, and myrrh *(Commiphora myrrha*) gum resin, and also about less dramatic medicinal herbs such as alfalfa (*Medicago sativa*) herb, chamomile (*Matricaria chamomila*) flower, mullein (*Verbascum thapsus*) leaf, and raspberry (*Rubus ideaus*) leaf. During one of my presentations, I called the less dramatic plants "wimpy" because their actions are usually neither as rapid nor as dramatic as heroic herbs. After the presentation, a woman came to me and questioned my calling such plants "wimpy" herbs. She suggested that I needed a name other than "wimpy" to describe their action on the body. I agreed with her that the word did not do justice to the healing properties of these herbs and promised her that I would find a new term.

I thought long and hard about the differences between heroic herbs and "wimpy" herbs. Heroic herbs certainly are stronger, more dramatic in their effectiveness, and generally are taken for shorter periods of time. The "wimpy" herbs, on the other hand, are usually slower to show their benefits and are usually not as dramatic in their effects. However, "wimpy" herbs are most often just as effective as heroic herbs. However, they often do so over time. It finally dawned on me that what "wimpy" herbs delivered consistently was nourishment to our tissues so that our bodies can function more effectively. I realized that these herbs feed our bodies in a manner similar to the way moms feed their sick children chicken soup and surround them with loving, tender attention to get them well. The herbs I referred to as "wimpy" were actually "nourishing" herbs. In effect, like food, they feed the core of who we are. From that day on, I changed my language to reflect my new awareness that these herbs were nourishing herbs. I am forever grateful that this woman took the time to help me realize how powerful nourishing herbs actually are and how they are far from wimpy.

Raspberry and blackberry belong to the nourishing category of plants. Both feed our tissues and bodies. Let's examine how these two herbs share their properties with us to support and heal human beings.

Pregnancy and Breast-Feeding

For hundreds of years, herbalists have recommended the use of raspberry leaves as a safe and reliable tea to promote a healthy pregnancy. The leaves are used to prepare the uterus for an easy labor and delivery. Additionally, raspberry leaf tea can be drunk liberally during the pregnancy as it helps alleviate nausea and reduce morning sickness. Contemporary herbalist Amanda McQuade-Crawford (1998) encourages expectant mothers to drink one cup of tea daily from the time of conception. For the last three months of pregnancy, she recommends raspberry leaf tea at the rate of two to three cups per day. She believes that this regimen helps to coordinate muscle contractions and promotes a delivery with fewer complications.

Some midwives have reported that giving the tea during labor helps to reduce the mother's exhaustion and strengthen without stimulating. If taken before delivery for several weeks or months, smaller doses during labor seem to synergize and coordinate efficient contractions. Because drinking cups of tea may not always be practical during labor, it can be made a day (or even three or so hours) ahead of time, frozen as ice cubes, and broken into small chips for the pregnant woman to chew, suck, or let melt in her mouth during the delivery. Mothers have indicated that the raspberry leaf tea as ice chips are remarkably refreshing during this intense period (McQuade 1998).

After delivery, raspberry or blackberry leaf tea stimulates the production and maintenance of breast milk and aids in returning the uterus to normal (a process called involution).

Recent Scientific Research Affirms Indications

Science is finally affirming what midwives have known for hundreds of years. In an *in-vitro* (test tube) experiment, when lack of tone was present in the isolated uterus, raspberry leaf caused stimulation of these tissues. Conversely, when the uterus was overly toned, raspberry leaf induced relaxation. Such observations suggest a regulatory action of raspberry leaves on uterine tone (Duke 2002). These seemingly opposite actions from an herb to tissues is what herbalists refer to as an *amphoteric action*.

In herbal medicine, an *amphoteric* herb is defined as an herb that normalizes the function or the activity of an organ or a system within the body. When a tissue or organ needs stimulation, an amphoteric herb specific for that organ or tissue will do just that. Conversely, when the same tissue or organ needs relaxation, the same amphoteric herb leads to relaxation. It's almost as if the herb knows how to affect the tissues or organs depending on the need.

A very small-scale pharmacological study conducted in 1941 reported that, in three pregnant women administered a raspberry extract, inappropriate uterine contractions decreased in frequency and strength. Secondary contractions (a negative effect during delivery) were also eliminated. The authors of the study noted that raspberry leaf may be useful for treating irregular uterine action during labor and menstruation (Bone 2003, Burn 1941).

In a retrospective study, mothers who used one to six cups of raspberry tea or one to eight tablets of powdered raspberry leaf daily during pregnancy showed no adverse effects from taking the herb. The results of this study suggest that raspberry leaf might decrease the likelihood of pre-term or post-term gestation. Additionally, women who used raspberry leaves were less likely to incur an artificial rupture of their membranes or require a caesarean section, forceps birth, or vacuum birth than women in the control group (Parsons 1999).

In a randomized, double-blind, placebo-controlled clinical trial that involved women who were followed from 32 weeks of pregnancy to labor, the women in the treatment group received 1.2 grams of raspberry leaf twice a day. No adverse effects on the infants or mothers were observed. Additionally, it was reported that slightly fewer women in the treatment group had forceps or vacuum-assisted birth (Simpson 2001).

Other Female Reproductive Health Issues

Raspberry and blackberry leaves are also used outside of the pregnancy sphere to promote female reproductive health. They are a tonifying treatment to the reproductive organs and help stimulate normal functions of these tissues. They are often recommended to help rebuild post-partum mothers who want to prepare for another childbirth. Raspberry leaves are suggested to young girls who are just beginning their menstrual cycles as well as to menopausal women wishing to prevent loss of tone in their reproductive organs as they age. Women with prolonged or heavy menstrual bleeding also benefit from raspberry leaves' astringent tannins and nourishing minerals, although the root cause for the bleeding should be addressed (McQuade-Crawford 1998). The leaves are an excellent support as an adjunctive treatment for excessive menstruation and as a general uterine tonic following surgery to the uterus, the removal of fibroids, the termination of pregnancy, or following a curettage (Trickey 1998).

Mineralizing Agent

The minerals present in the leaf tea make it a useful and quick strengthening beverage in cases of dehydration, imbalance of salts, or fatigue. In conjunction with other nourishing herbs such as oat (*Avena sativa*) straw, horsetail (*Equisetum arvense*) herb, alfalfa (*Medicago sativa*) herb, stinging nettle (*Urtica dioica*) herb, and red clover (*Trifolium pratense*) flower, raspberry and blackberry leaves are used to help increase the uptake of minerals from the gut. As the aging process occurs, the nails, hair, and bones become more brittle while the skin loses its elasticity. A tea blend like the one suggested above strengthens nails, hair, and bones. It also promotes the elasticity of the skin, especially if it is taken regularly over a long period of time (at least 6 months). Herbalists often suggest a tea made from these herbs as a regular supplement, just as nutritionists may recommend a multi-vitamin and mineral supplement. It has been speculated that the high silica and mineral content present in the tea may be what contributes to its efficacy.

Gastro-Intestinal System

One of the main constituents found in both raspberry and blackberry leaves and roots are tannins. Tannins are the constituents that give some herbs their astringency—that is, the ability to bind up or contract tissues. Tannins bind to the protein layer of the inflamed mucous membranes and cause them to thicken. This, in turn, slows the reabsorption of toxic materials into the gastro-intestinal tissues and restricts excessive gastro-intestinal secretions.

Prickly, red, wineberry cane and emerging leaves closeup. *Susan Belsinger*

Tannins also help to reduce the excess sensitivity of nerve endings in the gut.

One of the classic indications for raspberry and blackberry leaf infusion is mild to moderate chronic diarrhea. The tea from these two herbs does not disrupt the normal functioning of the stomach, but controls the irritation and inflammation in the small intestine (Ashok 2012). The same anti-inflammatory effects of tannins help to control all indications of gastritis, esophagitis, enteritis, and irritable bowel disorders. The decoction of the leaves is also used for mouth ulcerations, tonsillitis, and sore throats. In France, the dried leaves are reduced to a powder and approximately 10 grams (1/3 ounce) are added to water to stop diarrhea (Fournier 1948). It squelches indigestion and diarrhea. That's why it has an important role in children's health care, too, since it is safe for all ages (McQuade-Crawford 1998).

Tonsillitis and Sore Throats

Tonsillitis is an inflammation of the small round lymph glands called tonsils that sit on the sides of the throat and occurs most frequently in children under the age of nine. Commonly the tonsils become inflamed when they become infected with microorganisms such as *Streptococcus, Staphylococcus,* or viruses. Blackberry root, because of its high tannin content, was commonly used in an early American folk remedy for tonsillitis (Duke 1997). Blackberry root tea is usually used as a gargle or mouthwash because the root has a higher tannin content than the leaves. The root tea provides comfort to the person suffering from tonsillitis.

Blackberry root tea in conjunction with other herbs such as echinacea (*Echinacea angustifolia*) root, fresh elderberry (*Sambucus nigra*) fruit extract, and andrographis (*Andrographis paniculata*) herb is useful when a cold or flu settles in the throat.

Blackberry root tea is of great help when tonsillitis makes for painful and difficult swallowing. Not only does the root tea deliver anti-inflammatory properties, it also provides important antibacterial and antiviral properties.

Urinary System

Blackberry and raspberry root have been used for the relief of urethral irritation and to soothe the kidneys, urinary tract, and ducts (Hutchens 1973, McIntyre 1994). They are a mild diuretic and help to tone the kidneys and bladder. Both herbs contain small amounts of a constituent called *arbutin*, a substance that gently disinfects the urinary tract. Arbutin is a mild antiseptic as well as a soothing diuretic.

Skin Health

Raspberry or blackberry leaves are used externally as a compress for skin wounds or burns, sores, boils, eczema, psoriasis, raw skin surfaces, chronic skin conditions, skin ulcerations, and hemorrhoids. Tannins from the leaf decoction not only heal burns and stop bleeding, but they also stop infection while they continue to heal the wound internally. The ability of tannins to form a protective layer over the exposed or abraded tissue keeps the wound from becoming infected. Additionally, the precipitation of proteins of the exposed, damaged tissues stimulates the formation a scab and facilitates its healing (Ashok 2012).

Anticancer Properties

In the last 50 years, it has been suggested that raspberry and blackberry leaves possess significant anticancer properties (Fermeli 2016). Until recently, the exact mechanisms of this action had been eluding researchers. However, a group of constituents called hydrolysable tannins, found in the raspberry and blackberry genera, have been studied for their potential effects against cancer (Yang 2000, Gudj 2004, Tanimura 2005). James Duke, a former economic botanist for the USDA, asserts that the 10 to 12% tannins found in the leaves of raspberry and blackberry make its tea competitive with the better known and more publicized green tea (*Camellia sinensis*) as an anticancer agent. He states that he suspects that the wild strains of raspberry and blackberry may contain more of the anticancer polyphenols than the cultivated ones (Duke 1997).

Additionally, over the last few years, another group of constituents in this same phenolic family, ellagitannins, also found in these two herbs, has been investigated for its anticancer effects (Yidirim 2015, Ismail 2016). Furthermore, the fruits of both herbs have been shown to possess strong antioxidant effects. Drinking raspberry/blackberry leaf tea and eating the fruit of these two herbs on a regular basis will provide substantial amounts of these anticancer nutrients (Seeram 2006). Obviously, both the leaves and fruits are best obtained from an organic source.

Preparation and Dosage: Pour boiling water over 1.5 g (approximately 1 tablespoon) of the finely cut leaves, let sit for 10 to 15 minutes, then pass through a tea strainer. 1 teaspoon is equal to 0.6 grams. (Whitehouse 1941, Wichtl 1994). Raspberry and blackberry leaves are rather inexpensive as well as pleasant and/or fairly neutral in taste. Adding other herbs, such as spearmint (*Mentha spicata*) leaf, peppermint (*Mentha* x *piperita*) leaf, chamomile (*Matricaria chamomila*) flower, or lemon balm (*Melissa officinalis*) leaf, enhances the taste of these two herbs.

To make a tea, use 3 to 6 grams of the herb, 1 to 2 1/2 teaspoons per cup, up to 2 ounces per pint, infused ten to fifteen minutes, taken one cup two to three times a day. It can be made as strong as you like, but since the dried leaf is fluffy and lightweight, it's difficult to stuff much more than 2 ounces plus water into a teapot. Since there is no toxicity known, it can be taken liberally.

Tincture: 5 ml. per day, 1 teaspoon diluted in water one to three times a day. This convenient form may be used in 1/4 teaspoon doses as frequently as needed for morning sickness, though in the first trimester a strict policy of avoiding alcohol may be followed with 1/2 cup of strong tea sipped as often as needed (McQuade-Crawford 1998).

Safety in pregnancy and lactation: The American Herbal Products Association's *Botanical Safety Handbook* classifies the genus *Rubus* as "an herb that can be safely consumed when used appropriately" (Safety Class 1), and "an herb for which no clinically relevant interactions are expected" (Interaction Class A) (Gardner 2013). In a nutshell, no adverse effects are expected.

Contraindications: None known (Gardner 2013)

Side Effects: None known (Gardner 2013)

Drug and Supplement Interactions: None known (Gardner 2013)

Toxicity: None known (Gardner 2013)

References

Ashok, PK and K. Upadhyaya. 2012: Tannins are Astringent. *Journal of Pharmacognosy and Phytochemistry* 1(3): 45-50.

Bone, K. *A Clinical Guide to Blending Liquid Herbs.* Elsevier Churchill Livingstone, 2003.

Burn, JH. and Withell, ER. 1941. A principle in raspberry leaves which relaxes uterine muscle. *Lancet,* 2: 1-3.

Crellin, JK and J. Philpot. *A Reference Guide to Medicinal Plants.* Duke University Press, 1990.

"Raspberry." *Gerard's Herbal,* 112. Accessed 9/15/19. https://books.google

Duke, J. *The Green Pharmacy.* St. Martin's Paperbacks, 1997.

-----. *Handbook of Medicinal Herbs.* 2 ed. CRC Press, 2002.

Ferlemi, AV and FN Lamari. 2016. Berry leaves: an alternative source of bioactive natural products of nutritional and medicinal value. *Antioxidants.* 5: 17-37.

Fournier, P. *Le livre des plantes medicinales et vénéneuses de France.* 3 volumes. Editions Lechevalier, 1948.

Gardner, Z. and M. McGuffin, eds. *American Herbal Products Association's Botanical Safety Handbook.* 2 ed. CRC Press, 2013.

Gudej, J. and Tomczyk, M. 2004. Determination of flavonoids, tannins and ellagic acid in leaves from Rubus L. species. *Arch Pharm Res.* 27(11): 1114-1119.

Hutchens, A. *Indian Herbalogy of North America.* Merco, 1973.

Ismail, T., Calcabrinin, C., Diaz, AR., Figognari, C., Turrini, E., Catanrazo, E., Akhtar, S., and Sestili. P. 2016. Ellagitannins in cancer chemoprevention and therapy. *Toxins.* 8(5): 151+.

Kurschmann, GJ and JD Kirschmann. *Nutrition Almanac.* 4 ed. McGraw-Hill, 1996.

McIntyre, A. *The Complete Woman's Herbal.* Henry Holt Company, 1994.

McQuade-Crawford, *A Phytopharmacy and Materia Medica.* National College of Phytotherapy, 1998.

Parsons, M., Simpson, M. and Ponton, T. 1999. Raspberry leaf and its effect on labour: safety and efficacy. *Aust Coll Midwives* Inc J. 12(3): 20-25.

Seeram, NP., Adams, LS., Zhang, Y., Lee, R., Sand, D., Scheuller, HS., and Herber, D. 2006. Blackberry, Black Raspberry, Blueberry, Cranberry, Red Raspberry, and Strawberry Extracts Inhibit Growth and Stimulate Apoptosis of Human Cancer Cells In Vitro. *J. Agric. Food Chem.* 54(25): 9329-9339.

Simpson M, Parsons M, Greenwood J, Wade K. 2001. Raspberry leaf in pregnancy: its safety and efficacy in labor. *J Midwifery Womens Health* 46(2): 51-59.

Skenderi, G. *Herbal Vade Mecum.* Herbacy Press, 2003.

Tanimura, S., Kadomoto, R., Tanaka T., Zhang, YJ., Kouno, I., Kohno, M. 2005. Suppression of tumor cell invasiveness by hydrolyzable tannins (plant polyphenols) via the inhibition of matrix metalloproteinase-2/-9 activity. *Biochem. Biophys. Res. Commun.* 330(4): 1306–1313.

Trickey, R. *Women, Hormones & Menstrual Cycle.* St. Leonards, Australia: Allen & Unwin, 1998.

Van Hellemont, J. *Compendium de Phytotherapie.* Association Pharmaceutique Belge, 1986.

Whitehouse, B. 1941. Fragarine: an inhibitor of uterine action. *Br. med. J.,* 2: 370-371.

Wichtl, M. *Herbal Drugs and Phytopharmaceuticals.* CRC Press, 1994.

Woodward, M. *Gerard's Herball: The Essence thereof distilled by Marcus Woodward.* London, England; Spring Books, 1927.

Yang, LL., Lee, CY., Yen, KY. 2000. Induction of apoptosis by hydrolyzable tannins from Eugenia jambos L. on human leukemia cells. *Cancer Lett.* 157(1): 65–75.

Yildirim, I. and Kutlu, T. 2015. Anticancer Agents: Saponin and Tannin. *International Journal of Biological Chemistry.* 9(6): 332-340.

Daniel Gagnon is a Franco-Ontarian (Canada) who relocated to Santa Fe in 1979. He has been a practicing medical herbalist since 1976 and is the owner of Herbs, Etc., an herbal medicine retail store and manufacturing facility located in Santa Fe. In the summer time, he spends his free time in the garden where Mother Nature continues to teach him about the mystery of life. www.herbsetc.com.

Wineberries actually gleam when they are ripe. *Susan Belsinger*

Raspberry Medicine
Carol Little

Herbalists love this special perennial from the Rose family. Medicinally, from leaves to root to bark and berry, raspberry (*Rubus idaeus*) has been appreciated and used throughout the world for centuries, primarily as a uterine tonic. There is, though, much more to raspberry medicine, to be sure! I hope you'll enjoy this ramble through some of my favourite ways we can use this traditional medicine to heal and help us to live our best lives.

Highly Nutritive Tonic

Red raspberry leaves are rich in antioxidants, vitamins, and minerals. They provide vitamins B and C, calcium, potassium, magnesium, manganese, phosphorus, iron, and zinc. This deeply nutritive herb makes a good general tonic for children, helping to build strong teeth and bones. It can be helpful in formulas for childhood fevers as well. It has been used in all stages of a woman's life providing a rich supply of vitamins and minerals.

Raspberry leaves contain fragarine, several tannins, and polypeptides. The alkaloid fragarine, in concert with other con-stituents, tones and relaxes the uterine and pelvic muscles. The tannins help to alleviate diarrhea and can be a part of treatment for dysentery.

We can make infusions from either fresh or dried raspberry leaves. The tea is a refreshing beverage, enjoyed hot or chilled. Rosemary Gladstar, in her classes on Sage Mountain, Vermont, shared the following: "Raspberry leaf is one of the richest sources of iron, and can be used to replenish iron-poor blood, often combined with nettle for anemia and related low energy levels. It is also a rich source of niacin and manganese, a trace mineral used by the body to produce healthy connective tissue such as bone matrix and cartilage, and an important factor in energy metabolism. Use as a nutritive tonic when energy is low, when recovering from illness, and at times when an endocrine tonic is needed."

Raspberry Highlights: **Bolded** attributes are primary and powerful.

alterative
astringent
anti-catarrhal
anti-inflammatory
anti-emetic
carminative
diuretic
emmenagogue
hemostatic
nervine
parturient
uterine tonic
vulnerary

Astringent herbs are often used for skin conditions and imbalances of the digestive tract including:

- Infectious diarrhea
- Leg ulcers (e.g., diabetic and venous ulcers)
- Hemorrhoids
- Inflammatory bowel disease (e.g., ulcerative colitis)
- Stomach ulcers
- Wounds, cuts, abrasions, burns
- Esophagitis (inflammation or irritation of the esophagus due to acid reflux, bacterial or viral infections, or side effects from medications)

The astringency of raspberry leaf can help with mouth ulcers, sore throats, sore and infected gums, and tonsillitis too. To ease discomfort, make a strong raspberry leaf tea and allow to cool, then use as a gargle throughout the day. Alternatively, use a raspberry leaf tincture or a strong tea to dab on skin abrasions. Raspberry is also a vulnerary herb that can be very healing to the skin and helpful with wounds and rashes. It can also be very helpful in the treatment of conjunctivitis. Ayurvedic herbalist Anne McIntyre advises: "Raspberry leaves tone the mucus membranes throughout the entire body and soothe the kidneys and the urinary tract."

Raspberry leaf, as a **uterine tonic**, is used throughout women's lives to:

- help with menstrual cramps
- regulate menstrual periods
- strengthen the uterus

- prepare for childbirth
- support the mom-to-be during pregnancy
- avoid "threatened" miscarriage
- induce labour
- help shorten labour
- help with post-partum issues
- help to regulate hormones

According to Dr. Aviva Romm, one of my favourite women herbalists-turned-medical doctor: "Red raspberry leaf is a safe choice to help induce labor. It may be taken in a strong tea, prepared using 1/4 ounce (about 4 grams) of the dried herb to 1 pint of water, steeped for 20 minutes, and several cupfuls taken daily until labor commences. It is not associated with causing preterm labor and has been associated with decreased complications at birth for the mother and baby."

Finally, according to herbalist Susun Weed, "Raspberry leaf tea can alleviate nausea and morning sickness during pregnancy and may also prove beneficial in a plan to increase breast milk production." Weed suggests combining raspberry leaves with red clover blossoms (*Trifolium pratense*) to make an excellent fertility blend.

Here are some traditional formulas for specific situations. Unless otherwise noted, these formulae are derived from class notes from my classes with Director Michael Vertolli at the Living Earth School of Herbalism, Toronto, Ontario.

For Balancing Female Reproductive System

Specific herbs should be selected and customized to the needs of the individual, but a simple, general idea would be 4 parts raspberry leaf to 1 part vitex berries (*Vitex agnus-castus*) in tea or tincture form.

A lovely tea blend might include raspberry leaves, nettle leaves (*Urtica dioica*), red clover flowers, lady's mantle leaves (*Alchemilla vulgaris*), and vitex berries. Both Rosemary Gladstar and Michael Vertolli suggest that pregnant women in the first trimester can enjoy 2 to 3 cups of raspberry leaf infusion daily.

In cases of morning sickness, add carminative herbs without significant emmenagogue properties (herbs which stimulate blood flow in the pelvic area and uterus) such as spearmint (*Mentha spicata,*), lemon balm (*Melissa officinalis*) and lemongrass *(Cymbopogon citratus)*. Spearmint leaves added to raspberry tincture can be very helpful and are the best of these suggestions.

Morning Sickness Formula

Raspberry leaf	30 to 50%
Spearmint leaf	30 to 50%
Ginger or Cinnamon	5 to 10%

This morning sickness tea formula should not be taken more than 4 times daily. Make it with fresh or dried plants.

Drink raspberry leaf tea, combined with dried partridgeberry (*Mitchella repens*) for the second and third trimesters. Some herbalists also combine with nettle leaf and milky oat tops *(Avena sativa)*. The goal here is to nourish the mother-to-be with deeply nutritive foods and provide additional toning and support to the uterus and reproductive system overall.

Here's a good tea formula for the first pregnancy, women with a history of long labour, or women who have had abortions or miscarriages. Ginger is optional but sometimes very helpful. Combine for a nourishing tea.

Pregnancy formula

Raspberry leaves	70%
Partridgeberry	20 to 30%
Ginger root, if using	3 to 5%

If labour is late, traditional herbal formulas include partridgeberry and blue cohosh root (*Caulophyllum thalictroides*) or black cohosh root (*Cimicifuga racemosa/Actaea racemosa)* in varying percentages which increase the intensity and frequency of contractions, relax the uterus, help to dilate the cervix, and contribute to a less painful birth experience. Uterine stimulants, uterine relaxants, and uterine tonics make up these formulae. Raspberry leaf is a big part of these. Consult your local herbalist and/or midwife about these formulas, which are typically customized to match each woman's needs and specific situation. Studies at Westmead Hospital in Australia in 1998 show that use of raspberry leaf can definitely shorten and improve a woman's labour.

After birth, herbalists sometimes suggest something like this post-partum formula to help to contract the uterus and expel the placenta as well as help the new mother cope with any anxiety, mood swings and hormonal imbalances. The formula is primarily a nervine formula with a uterine component. It can be made into a tea or a tincture, though the tea is recommended for nursing mothers.

Post-Partum Formula

Raspberry leaf	20%
Lemon balm leaf	25%
Motherwort herb	25%
Blackhaw	20%
Ginger root	10%

Dose: 2 to 3 cups of tea or 4 to 5 droppers, 3 to 4 times a day for 3 to 4 weeks after the birth. It is best not to take this formula for longer than a month as it can interfere with the hormones necessary for milk production. Note: supportive gentle anti-depressant herbs can be added if indicated.

Grow your own or purchase good quality dried raspberry leaves to make your infusions and tinctures. I normally buy my supply from IHA members Andrea and Matthias Reisen of Healing Spirits Herb Farm, Avoca, New York. In conversation with these two amazing herbalists recently, they advised that they have had good results working with raspberry medicine for men too. Andrea mentioned that she uses both tinctures and teas and that the effect is similar for men: toning and nourishing for the sexual organs. She has used raspberry leaf in combination with ginkgo, hawthorn and red clover in varying formulae.

I hope that the powers of Raspberry Medicine will encourage everyone to take another look at this special plant, which offers so much to everyone. It seems that raspberry leaf can add good support to us in every stage of life. Here's to telling the world about it!

Please note, it's very important to recognize that the information in this article is intended for educational purposes only and should not be considered as a recommendation or an endorsement of any particular medical or health treatment. We recommend that you consult with a qualified healthcare practitioner before using herbal products, particularly if you are pregnant, nursing, or on any medications. This information is not intended to diagnose, treat, cure, or prevent any disease.

References

Boon, Heather and Michael Smith. *50 Most Common Medicinal Herbs.* Robert Rose Inc., 1994.

Class notes from "Women's Reproductive Health." Herbal apprenticeship with Rosemary Gladstar. September, 1997.

Class notes from "Materia Medica" from Michael Vertolli R.H., at Living Earth School of Herbalism, Toronto, Ontario. 2001 https://www.livingearthschool.ca.

Gladstar, Rosemary. *Herbal Healing for Women.* Fireside Books, 1993.

-----. *Rosemary Gladstar's Family Herbal.* Story Books, 2001.

McIntyre, Anne. *The Complete Woman's Herbal.* Henry Holt and Company, 1995.

Reisen, Matthias and Andrea. Personal interview. June 2019. Healing Spirits Herb Farm, Avoca, NY. www.healingspiritsherbfarm.com.

Romm, Aviva M.D. "5 Safe Herbs for a More Comfortable Pregnancy." Accessed 8/1/19. https://avivaromm.com/5-safe-herbs-for-a-more-comfortable-pregnancy-and-better-birth/.

Weed, Susun. *Childbearing Years.* Ash Tree, 1986.

Carol Little, R.H., is a traditional herbalist in Toronto, Canada, where she has a private practice working primarily with women. Her easy-to-digest weekly blog posts offer quick takeaway ideas to help readers feel their best (www.studiobotanica.com). Carol is a current professional and past board member of the Ontario Herbalists Association. She combines her love of travel and passion for all things green to write about both. Carol has written for *Vitality Magazine* and the monthly online *Natural Herbal Living Magazine.* She is a regular contributor to *Home Herbalist* (http://homeherbalist.net/) as well as the annual Herb of the Year™ books. Two of her recipes appear in Rosemary Gladstar's *Fire Cider: 101 Zesty Recipes for Health-Boosting Remedies* (2019). Check out her active Facebook community at www.facebook.com/studiobotanica and follow her on Instagram www.instagram.com/studiobotanica.

Raspberry Soother Balm
Marge Powell

When we think of ripe and sweet red raspberries (*Rubus idaeus*) and their cousin black raspberries (*Rubus occidentalis*), our associations are usually culinary rather than cosmetic. Indeed, one of the bothersome things about eating these raspberries would be those annoying little seeds. But, when cold-pressed, those annoying little seeds yield oils that are amazing helpers for our bodies and especially our skin.

Red raspberry seed oil offers the anti-aging benefits of improving skin elasticity, suppleness, and flexibility while softening and smoothing the look of wrinkles, fine lines, and sagging skin. In addition, it is hydrating, antioxidant, and has lipid-barrier-forming characteristics.

In a study published in 2000, B. David Oomah and his associates found that raspberry seed oil:

- Is very high in the antioxidant vitamin E which is important in preventing oxidative damage which can lead to skin cancer and premature skin aging. It is also high in the carotenoid vitamin A.

- Has a high level of essential fatty acids, primarily linoleic and linolenic acids. The alpha linolenic acid content is the highest found in any fruit seed oil. The high level of linolenic acid along with a high phytosterol content makes the oil anti-inflammatory and can be an aid in the struggle with eczema, psoriasis, and rosacea.

- Can keep skin moisturized because the high levels of phytosterols reduce trans-epidermal water loss.

- Can help repair damaged skin, especially from the sun, again because of the high phytosterol content.

- Contains ellegic acid, an antioxidant, which reduces the destruction of collagen and inflammatory response, both of which are a major cause of wrinkles.

* Absorbs UVB and UVC and provides limited protection from UVA. It may be a broad-spectrum UV protectant but further studies are needed to verify this.

Red raspberry seed oil improves skin elasticity, reduces wrinkles, dryness, and skin lines, and regenerates skin cells. It also has omega 3 and 6 fatty acids which have been shown to improve acne and dermatitis. The ellagic acids show antibacterial activity which is not only helpful for acne sufferers but soothes skin lesions, rashes, rosacea, and eczema. It is not likely to clog pores and continued use will balance the oil production of the skin.

Black raspberries (*R. occidentalis*) contain many of the same health protecting compounds as their red cousins, but they also contain high levels of anthocyanins. Some studies have demonstrated that black raspberries may have even stronger antioxidant properties than red raspberries. A study published in the June 2002 issue of the *Journal of Agricultural and Food Chemistry* reported that among the tested cane berries (berries of the *Rubus* species), black raspberries were the winner in terms of antioxidant capacity. The other tested berries showing high levels of antioxidants included red raspberries (*R. idaeus*), evergreen blackberries (*R. laciniatus*), marionberries (*R. ursinus*), and boysenberries (*R. ursinus* x *idaeus)*.

It is not likely that many of us have access to the equipment required to express these seed oils so we must rely on purchased oils. A word of caution: *always* check the Latin name of the berry used in the oil. Some producers call black raspberry seed oil "blackberry oil." The different *Rubus* varieties have differing qualities. The berries being discussed here are *Rubus idaeus* (red raspberries) and *Rubus occidentalis* (black raspberries).

The color of both raspberry oils I have used is slightly yellow with just the faintest earthy scent. But other oils from other producers may be clear, yellow, or have a greenish tint. The oils are absorbed into the skin at a medium rate and I do not find that they leave an oily residue but rather a silky feel. They are generally not the primary ingredient in a formulation but are used in smaller quantities. They have a shelf life of about 2 years, and I suggest they should be refrigerated. They are readily available on the internet and are moderately priced with a cost for 4 ounces between $20 and $25. But, again, it is critical that you pay attention to the Latin name of the berry the producer is using. If you have an allergy to any type of berries, proceed with caution and do a test on a small patch of skin before introducing raspberry seed oils into your life.

If you are browsing the internet for raspberry seed oils, you may notice the high prices for products made with these oils for very small quantities. The following formula is easy to follow and you can create it with higher quality ingredients than most products available commercially, especially if you use organic oils. The resulting skin balm is thicker than a lotion and can be used as a night cream or as a facial balm. However, your skin will welcome it wherever you apply it.

When creating a formula, it is important that all the ingredients support your objective. The objective of this formula is both to deliver anti-aging effects and to heal and soothe damaged skin, so the properties of each ingredient are listed behind that ingredient.

You will need:

- A scale to weigh the oils
- A pan to heat the oils
- Alcohol (IPA 70%) in a spray bottle or with a clean soft cloth
- Small jars with lids
- A small funnel to assist in filling the jars
- Thermometer

Raspberry Soother Balm

For scent, I chose rose and patchouli essential oils for their anti-aging properties. However, rose is expensive and patchouli is not tolerated by some. Viable substitutes would be rose geranium essential oil or lavender essential oil. Regarding the carrier oils, avocado oil is therapeutic and healing; it contains protein, amino acids, and large amounts of vitamins A, B, D, and E, and the glycerides of many fatty acids. It is easily absorbed by the skin, regenerates skin cells, and softens tissues. It is the most nourishing oil (along with wheat germ oil) and the most penetrating (along with hazelnut oil). Almond oil softens, smooths, and conditions skin. Rich in protein, this nourishing emollient helps relieve itching from eczema. Wheat germ oil, a natural antioxidant, is vitamin-rich with high levels of vitamin E plus carotene and vegetable lecithin which nourishes skin cells and hinders moisture loss. It is especially good for dry skin, helps healing, and reduces scarring from wounds and acne. Jojoba is really a wax that is indigestible to bacteria. It is good for acne because it dissolves sebum and makes the skin feel satin smooth. Vitamin E oil is a preservative. When choosing beeswax, use local beeswax, if possible. It should not be white, which is an indication of having been bleached, but should be a warm, brown color.

3 ounces avocado oil
3 ounces almond oil
1 ounce red raspberry seed oil
1 ounce black raspberry seed oil
2 ounces wheat germ oil
1 ounce jojoba
.6 ounces vitamin E oil
1.8 ounces beeswax
1 ounce rose essential oil in jojoba
.2 ounces patchouli essential oil

Spray the funnel, the interior of the saucepan, and the bottles and their lids with alcohol then let dry. If not using a sprayer, dampen a cloth with the alcohol and wipe the funnel, the interior of the saucepan, and the bottles and their lids with alcohol.

In a saucepan, heat all of the oils and jojoba with the beeswax over low heat, until the beeswax melts (165°); let cool to 140° then add the rose in jojoba and patchouli essential oil and stir to incorporate.

Pour into the jars using the funnel; cover with the lids. Let cool to room temperature.

Clean any drips on the jars with alcohol. Label with the ingredients and date.

Freshly poured Raspberry Soother Balm. *Marge Powell*

Sealed and labeled Raspberry Soother Balm. *Marge Powell*

References

Oomah, Dave B., Stephanie Ladet, David V Godfrey, Jun Liang, and Benoit Girard. "Characteristics of raspberry (Rubus idaeus L.) seed oil." *Food Chemistry.* Volume 69, Issue 2. 1 May 2000. 187-193.

Marge Powell has been an herbalist for over 30 years and an avid plant person her entire life. Her herbal interests span the culinary, the medicinal, and body care aspects as well as growing herbs. She completed a medicinal herbal apprenticeship with Susun Weed and was introduced to herbal body care in workshops by Rosemary Gladstar.

Marge is a passionate cook and most of her cooking is herb-enhanced. She teaches classes in cooking with herbs, making your own medicines, creating lotions and ointments, making soap, and blending scents. She has conducted hands-on work-shops on these and other herbal topics across the United States. In 2000 she incorporated Magnolia Hill Soap Co., Inc. (www.magnoliahillsoaps.com) and in 2011 she added Magnolia Hill Nursery which wholesales organic herbs and heirloom vegetables to local garden centers.

She is currently a board member of the International Herb Association (IHA) and the International Herb Association Foundation and is past president of IHA's former Southeastern Region. She has had numerous herbal articles published in IHA's annual Herb of the Year™ publications.

Rubus leaves ready for picking in the briar patch. *Susan Belsinger*

In the Briar Patch with Blackberry

Andrea and Matthias Reisen

*I love to go out in late September
among the fat, overripe, icy, black blackberries
to eat blackberries for breakfast.*
Galway Kinnell, "Blackberry Eating"

Cultivated for centuries, *Rubus* fruits such as raspberry, blackberry, boysenberry—there over 200 types—can be defined as functional foods because of their protective and enhancing effects on health. These fruits have strong antioxidant, anti-inflammatory, antidiabetic, and anticarcinogenic properties against various cancer types. Their health-protecting effects are due to their various bioactive components, mainly high amounts of anthocyanins, giving those blue, red, and purple colors to berries which differ from other fruits.

We have all of these growing on our land. Some we have planted, but some are growing wild on the land just before the woods. Harvesting at the edge of the woods is our favorite, even though it is more difficult. There are always more briars to get through, usually very uneven ground, and, if you are not careful, a steep bank to fall down. But there are also bird nests to find, different birds to listen to, and their songs to try and make a story out of. We have squirrels and chipmunks to watch, and usually a few deer to watch, or watch them watching us. They seem to know we are harmless to them, and we delight in their presence. Last year we discovered a big, old, hollowed-out tree that had a family of flying squirrels (five young ones) living in it. As much as we enjoyed watching them, they did not like us so close. It is also a time to notice which plants are moving into the area and which ones seem to be receding; there is always a change going on. We meander along finally getting some berries or leaves in our basket, feeling like all is right in the world.

We have a juicer-steamer that we put on the stove, fill it up with all different berries, and make juice. We love that the juice comes out hot enough to put in jars; it self-seals and we have the memories of summer walks all winter long. We will also make jelly out of the juice in the winter when we have more time.

Historically, red raspberry leaf is perhaps one of the most venerated herbal uterine tonics. It is used during pregnancy to strengthen the uterus, improve labor outcome, and prevent excessive bleeding after birth. Its use continues to be highly popular. When we harvest the leaves, we use gloves and just run our hands up the stem. You will have a nice handful of leaves in your hand. It is an easy leaf to dry, as it has very little moisture. Myself, I drink at least a cup of tea a week, even though my childbearing days are far behind me. I feel this helps to nourish my uterus and keeps it happy.

Blackberry, usually a prickly fruit-bearing bush of the genus *Rubus*, is known for its dark edible fruits. Native chiefly to north temperate regions, wild blackberries are particularly abundant in eastern North America. We grow them on our farm for our own use. No matter how many bushes we plant, or how much they spread, we never seem to have enough. We wander by as we are working, and just graze on them as we go about our day. They also grow on the Pacific coast and are cultivated in many areas of North America and Europe. Blackberries are a fairly good source of iron, vitamin C, and antioxidants. They are generally eaten fresh, in preserves, or in baked goods such as cobblers and pies. We have strawberries, red raspberries and blackberries on our cereal most mornings.

We also use the blackberry root for diarrhea. We haven't found anything that works better, which is very helpful to know about if you are out camping in the woods. Brew up a nice cup of tea, and the world is easier again.

Blackberry (or any *Rubus*) Cordial: Fill a jar with berries, but do not pack down. Pour in enough vodka so that the berries are completely covered. Seal the jar. Let the jar stand for 2 months, shaking the jar every week. The vodka will color deeply. Strain the liquid through a metal sieve, and then through a coffee filter to remove the fruit. Add about 1 cup honey (more or less to taste) and stir until dissolved. Pour into pretty bottles. Drink as a cordial, or use in times of dire need.

Wineberry leaves, with silvery-white underside. *Susan Belsinger*

Andrea and Matthias Reisen have been community herbalists for over 30 years, co-founding Healing Spirits Herb Farm and Education Center located in Wallace, New York. Healing Spirits Herb Farm has been producing high quality certified organic medicinal herbs, both fresh and dry, for shipment throughout the United States and some foreign countries. Andrea has created their line of valued products under the Healing Spirits label. Both are former Peace Corp volunteers in the Philippines. They have studied numerous body therapies and are certified Zero Balancing Therapists. Andrea and Matthias have encouraged many farmers to consider herb growing and working with the land in new and different ways. Matthias works with Farmer-to-Farmer organizations and has volunteered for projects in Nepal, Belarus, Jamaica, Colombia, and the Dominican Republic. Together they have raised five children; there are three generations living on the farm. Their goal is to live and work in balance and harmony with Mother Nature and humankind.

Wineberry (*R. phoenicolasius*) with hairy, prickly calyces. *Susan Belsinger*

Pay Attention to *Rubus:* She Wants to Help!

Jane Hawley Stevens

Rubus wants my attention! She is waving at me with her open handed, palmate leaves, and grabbing me with her thorns as I walk by.

Pausing, I hear the warblers and crickets sing. I am grateful for this moment to stop and pay attention to my world, instead of hurrying to whatever it is I should do next. Breathing in the oxygen, perhaps created by *Rubus*' photosynthesis, I feel blessed, surrounded by an apothecary full of vitamins, minerals, and constituents growing along the way.

I am especially inspired when a plant offers wellness in more than one botanical part. *Rubus* gives us delicious, antioxidant, health-promoting fruits, with tannins in the leaf, bark, and roots, which have shown anti-inflammatory, toning activity.

Wild raspberry (*R. idaeus*) is best known for its fruits, but its leaves and roots have been revered by herbalists as a uterine tonic. Every herbal book on pregnancy recommends raspberry leaf tea. Good thing it is delicious and blends well in almost any herbal tea mixture. Any of the various *Rubus* species will act similarly, but Rosemary Gladstar insists that there is more benefit in the wild plants than the cultivated. Raspberry leaf is slightly sweet and astringent. The strong infusion reminds me of black tea, carrying a sufficient quantity of tannins to offer the nice pucker that comes with a good cup of Earl Grey tea. As Juliette de Barcli Levy says, "It would be rare for a Gypsy woman to go through pregnancy without having taken raspberry leaf tea…and the true Gypsy gives birth to her children with the ease of the wild vixen."

As I was a budding herbalist, wondering how one herb could do so much, I pondered the astringency in raspberry leaf. How could this help tone a uterus?

I visualized a large sponge, just emerging from a bucket of water. Imagine squeezing it out. The sponge looks more "toned" after squeezing out the extra water and can perform more like it should. This is the action *Rubus* offers as herbal tea on the uterus. No wonder women, before and after pregnancy, make a brew of this tea for smooth transitions. I see the tissues of a saturated organ gently massaged into a firmer form, better able to perform its functions.

Raspberry leaf is loaded with vitamins and minerals, too. It helps to maintain strong bones and cartilage, being one of the richest botanical sources of iron, niacin, manganese, and selenium. Raspberry leaves contain *fragarine*, a constituent that has an affinity for the pelvic muscles. What an ally raspberry leaf infusion is for new mothers, adding blood-building, absorbable iron and a toning quality to the uterus after childbirth. It is also used in the case of excessive bleeding during menstruation.

Astringent herbs like *Rubus* have qualities to fill an open prairie! They are used to bind and tone tissues. Astringent herbs are often considered antimicrobial, with the action of tightening the tissues. This makes it more difficult for pathogens to travel through the body, slowing the infection process while the body can build up immunity. Tissue toning can be utilized by regulating permeability-reducing discharge, as in the case of diarrhea, bleeding, and excess mucus. Astringents are also used for any inflammation of the mouth and throat. I use the astringent and potent *Salvia officinalis*, common sage, effectively for this condition. Other uses include reducing cankers and hemorrhaging. Besides raspberry leaf, other astringent herbs are *Geranium maculatum*, wild geranium; *Agrimonia eupatoria*, agrimony; *Salvia officinalis*, common sage; and *Alchemilla vulgaris*, ladies' mantle.

Raspberry is a member is the Rosaceae family, and has five petals, five sepals, and five stamens. There are usually five leaflets per leaf, but can vary from three to seven. The energy of five in Chinese medicine holds the energy of change. This is reflected in the leaflets, almost looking like the spokes of a wheel. This would be considered an example of the Doctrine of Signatures, of the plant giving a clue to how it is useful in its phenotype, or appearance, taking into account the surroundings and colors of the plant. The cycles of the uterus certainly represent changes in the life of a woman.

The fruit of raspberry is not a true berry, but aggregates of drupelets. A berry is actually a fleshy fruit without a stone produced from a single flower containing one ovary. The raspberry is technically an aggregate of several berries—surprise! Hand someone a raspberry and say, "Care for some raspberries?" and you would be correct!

Rubus species are ruled by the planets Mars and Pluto, under the sign of Scorpio. Scorpio rules the reproductive organs, so is beneficial to *Rubus*' leafy portions. Other herbs in this category are cramp bark, *Viburnum opulus* or *V. trilobum*, and pennyroyal, *Mentha pulegium.* Keep in mind, however, that pennyroyal is a powerful emmenagogue and should *not* be used during pregnancy!

Antioxidant-rich berries fortify the blood and fall under the ruling planet of sensual Virgo. Virgo is not a fruitful sign, representing the virgin, but represents the maiden who manages her own time while consciously nurturing earth and all beings. She is a symbol of autumn and harvest, the energy of collecting all to serve all, while paying full attention to detail. Try harvesting raspberries, blackberries, or black caps under the ruling planet of Virgo and see if any hidden subtleties happen!

Virgo is an Earth sign and rules the digestive system and stomach. This accentuates the tannins and bitter aspects of *Rubus* leaves. Tannins have a toning quality to tissues. Bitters make digestive juices flow for increased digestion and for better assimilation of vitamins and minerals.

Guided by the moon's influence in agricultural pursuits, harvest *Rubus* leaves under the moon sign of Capricorn, holding the energy of the sturdy goat and horns. Capricorn rules farms and productive gardens. Make *Rubus* jams under the Pisces moon, holding energy inward. Canning in general is favored under a Cancer moon, as summer comes into full swing and holds the energy of a crab, covered by a hard shell, protecting the contents.

Raspberry Leaf Infusion

When making a raspberry leaf tea, I like to add other nutritive and flavorful herbs. Some other nutritive herbs, high in vitamins and minerals, are *Medicago sativa,* alfalfa; *Taraxacum officinale*, dandelion leaf and root; *Urtica dioica*, nettles; *Echinacea purpurea*, echinacea or purple coneflower; and *Equisetum arvense*, horsetail.

My favorite flavoring herbs for teas are *Melissa officinalis*, lemon balm; any type of *Mentha* spp., mints; and *Ocimum sanctum,* tulsi or holy basil.

Pick a cup of fresh leaves or put 1/4 cup of dried leaves into a quart jar. Any other flavorful or nutritive herbs can be added. Boil water and pour over herbs. Seal the jar and steep for ten minutes for the tannins, four hours to overnight to extract the minerals. Two to four cups taken daily can make a positive shift in your system.

Nature has so many ways to improve our well-being. Take time to appreciate and engage in your natural surroundings. All the senses can be stimulated to bring in joy with a walk in nature: breathing in fresh oxygen, bringing clarity to the mind, noticing the color of the sky and surrounding plants, hearing the sounds of birds or breezes. Taste some familiar plants and see if you can determine some of their qualities; is it bitter, astringent, salty, sour, or pungent?

Picking some raspberry leaves to make a nice cup of tea upon your return home is a bonus. Putting yourself into the abundance of nature places you in a place of gratitude and security. Take that feeling and move it forward making the world a better place for all living things

References

De Baircli Levy, Juliette. *Common Herbs for Natural Health*, 2 ed. Ash Tree, 1997.

Gladstar, Rosemary. *Family Herbal: A Guide to Living Life with Energy, Health and Vitality*. Storey, 2001.

Beauty and joy began in 1982 when herbs first cultivated **Jane Hawley Stevens,** formulator and farmer. With a degree in horticulture from the University of Wisconsin-Madison, she founded her business in 1987 after creating public and private herb gardens. Four Elements Organic Herbals is based on plants grown in her cultivated fields, Chakra Garden, prairie and woodlands.

A pioneer of the organic farming movement and natural products industry, Jane inspires others through increasing people's connection to nature as a source of well-being through her products and classes in herbalism and organic living. Jane Hawley Stevens has been named the MOSES 2020 Organic Farmer of the Year. Visit her store in North Freedom, Wisconsin or go to www.fourelementsherbals.com.

Thicket of flowering raspberry bushes. *Susan Belsinger*

Height of summer, wineberries beneath wide leaves. *Susan Belsinger*

Bios for Illustrators and Photographers

Susan Belsinger—see bio on page 27.

Gert Coleman—see bio on page 67.

Peter Coleman grows trees, herbs, vegetables and at-risk plants in Middlefield, New York. A Master Gardener, Peter photographs woods, trees, streams, plants, and the world from social, political, and historical perspectives.

Davy Dabney—see bio on page 70.

Karen England—see bio on page 206.

Pat Kenny—see bio on page 27.

Bonny Lundy has taught Drawing Experimental Watercolor, Beginning Watercolor, and Flowering Watercolor for thirty-six years. Known mainly for painting bold florals and still life, winter and autumn woodlands, streams and mountains, she also enjoys painting seascapes, marshes, and abstract experimental work. With her strong love of nature and other cultures, Bonny has led workshops to Europe, the Caribbean and throughout the United States. Pleasant View Studio in Brookeville, Maryland, is her creative base, whose peaceful woodland and gardens provide great creative opportunities. Bonny looks forward to many more years of discovery in nature. www.BonnyLundy.com

Alicia Mann is a classically trained artist and metalsmith at Heritage Metalworks, LTD, in Downington, PA. She graduated from Maryland Institute College of Art. She integrates her interests in art and horticulture by growing flowers, herbs, vegetables, and fruit trees. Alicia's charming illustrations introduce the five sections of this book. ammann1212@gmail.com

Cooper T. Murray—see bio on page 135.

Diann Nance—see bio on page 140.

Karen O'Brien—see bio on page 216.

Marge Powell—see bio on page 259.

Stephanie Rose—see bio on page 148.

Jane Taylor—see bio on page 180.

Alice Tangerini, staff illustrator for the Botany Department at the National Museum of Natural History, Smithsonian Institution, has been specializing in drawing plants since 1972 in pen and ink, graphite, and recently digital color. Her illustrations appear in scientific periodicals, floras, and nature books. Alice teaches classes on illustration techniques and juried shows and presents lectures on illustration in botanical gardens and in academic institutions. She also manages and curates an extensive collection of botanical illustrations in the Botany Department: http://collections.mnh.si.edu/search/botany.

Pam Trickett grew up in Chicago, but relished days on the farm where her favorite dish was her grandma's wild blackberry cobbler. After college she and her husband migrated to upstate New York to teach. There she met an amazing herbalist and began taking workshops. She fell in love with growing, cooking with, and drawing herbs. Now happily retired, she enjoys painting landscapes and flowers, writing when the Muse visits, and volunteering. Despite the challenges of moles, voles, slugs, ticks, and deer, she still digs in the dirt.

Gail Wood Miller draws and paints for fun. She coaches women and children in holistic health, and writes and speaks on her research. She is a retired professor of English and humanities, living in Manhattan with her husband. Her art training includes the Wiesbaden Herzfeld School of Art, Cooper Union, and Spring Street Drawing Studio. She is a member of the Muscenetcong Watercolor Group, New Jersey.

Cover Credits

Front Cover

Background image: Pail full of just-picked, wild-foraged wineberries (*R. phoenicolasius*). *Susan Belsinger*

Back Cover:

Left: *Rubus* infusions: ruby-hued shrub, cordial, and vinegars. *Susan Belsinger*

Middle: Wineberry flowers. *Susan Belsinger*

Right: Plump, fresh picked blackberries. *Susan Belsinger*

Section Illustrations:

Alicia Mann's illustrations grace the section introductions on pages 1, 52, 88, 182, and 224.

Celebrating 25 Years of Herb of the Year™!

How the Herb of the Year™ is Selected

Every year since 1995, the International Herb Association has chosen an Herb of the Year™ to highlight. The Horticultural Committee evaluates possible choices based on their being outstanding in at least two of the three major categories: medicinal, culinary, or decorative. Many other herb organizations support the herb of the year selection and we work together to educate the public about these herbs during the year.

Herbs of the Year™: Past, Present and Future

1995	Fennel	2011	Horseradish
1996	Monarda	2012	Rose
1997	Thyme	2013	Elderberry
1998	Mint	2014	Artemisia
1999	Lavender	2015	Savory
2000	Rosemary	2016	Capsicum
2001	Sage	2017	Cilantro & Coriander
2002	Echinacea	2018	Humulus
2003	Basil	2019	Agastache
2004	Garlic	2020	Rubus
2005	Oregano & Marjoram	2021	Parsley
2006	Scented Geraniums	2022	Violet
2007	Lemon Balm	2023	Ginger
2008	Calendula	2024	Yarrow
2009	Bay Laurel	2025	Chamomile
2010	Dill		

Books available on www.iherb.org

Join the IHA

Associate with other herb businesses and like-minded folks, network and have fun while you are doing it!

Membership Levels:

$500	Sponsor
$100	Business/Professional
$25	Additional member from your business
$100	Individual/Hobbyist
$25	Full-time Student
$30	Educator
$50	Small Business Start-up (first year of membership)

Log onto www.iherb.org to see what we are all about!

Membership includes:

Your business information listed on www.iherb.org
Membership directory
Herb of the Year™ publication
Quarterly newsletters
Online herbal support
Discounts on conference fees
Promotional support for IHA's Herb of the Year program and National Herb Week
Support for National Herb Day
Assocation with a network of diverse herbal businesses

www.ingramcontent.com/pod-product-compliance
Lightning Source LLC
Chambersburg PA
CBHW062021290426
44108CB00024B/2733